21st century gay

21st century

g

a

y

JOHN MALONE

M Evans
Lanham • New York • Boulder • Toronto • Plymouth, UK

M Evans
An imprint of Rowman & Littlefield
4501 Forbes Boulevard, Suite 200
Lanham, Maryland 20706
www.rowman.com

10 Thornbury Road, Plymouth PL6 7PP
United Kingdom

Distributed by
NATIONAL BOOK NETWORK

Book design and typesetting by Rik Lain Schell

Printed in the United States of America

For Paul Baldwin, with Love and Gratitude.

Contents

one

A Community of Many Parts

Some historical events pass into legend as great turning points despite their modest and somewhat confused origins. Every school child, for example, learns that the Boston Tea Party of 1773 was the beginning of the America Revolution—Samuel Adams led a group of Massachusetts colonists disguised as Mohawk Indians aboard three British vessels anchored in Boston Harbor and threw their cargo of heavily taxed tea overboard. But this is really just a convenient dramatic peg on which to hang the story of an increasing restiveness that had been growing in the colonies for some time. The American gay community has its own Boston Tea Party: the riot that erupted in the small hours of June 28, 1969, outside a gay bar called the Stonewall Inn in New York City's Greenwich Village. Appropriately enough, costuming played as much a part in 1969 as in 1773, but this time the revolutionaries were young men dressed in drag, and their protest was forced upon them rather than planned.

The Stonewall Inn, at 53 Christopher Street, was hardly the most prepossessing of New York's gay bars. I had been living in New York, on West 82nd Street, since my return from four years in Europe in November of 1965. Although I quite often joined friends for supper at the Lion's Inn, the cheap-but-good little restaurant next door on Christopher Street, I had been to the Stonewall Inn only once. You had to sign in at the door of the Stonewall as part of the ruse that it was a private club; the premises were dark, dingy and a little smelly, and the mix of types that frequented it—very giggly young boys, button-down preppies being daring, and a scattering of semi-drag queens and hippies—didn't turn me on. I was much more likely to go to Julius's, also in the Village, or the uptown Uncle Ty's on Third Avenue in the 80s. These were places where you could have a decent conversation with someone—whether you ended up going home with them or not. I was thirty, had broken things off with a lover of six year's standing, and was hoping to meet someone else I could have a settled relationship with.

But I heard about the riot at the Stonewall from a friend who lived in the Village the next afternoon, and that evening we paused in Sheridan Square to gawk at the milling mix of gays and straights that had gathered to see if anything else would happen. We were long gone before another confrontation erupted between gays and the police, with even more people getting clubbed by the cops this second night. At the time, the trouble on Christopher Street didn't seem terribly important. Indeed, few gays outside New York City heard anything about it. Accounts of the original riot on the 28th were muddled at the time, and no gay historian has even been able to pin down who started the taunting rubbish battle with the police officers who had raided the bar that night, as they did periodically. So many different stories have been told that the truth has been completely obscured by a kind of *Rashomon* effect, although it is generally agreed that it was the drag queens who were the angriest and most physical of the gay combatants.

At the time there was a lot of talk among gays about why the police, especially those in the Village, were so intent on raiding gay bars. It was known that Mayor John Lindsay had quietly ordered the police to stop posing as gays in order to entrap men who tried to pick them up in public toilets. The subway "tea rooms," as they were routinely referred to, thus became a major venue for picking up a trick in the middle of the day, as well as for on-the-spot blow-jobs. The bar raids were seen by many as police retaliation for having their entrapment fun and games curtailed. And that made the gay community angry. There were more than enough murders, burglaries, street hold-ups and other crimes going on to keep the police busy. But a lot of officers—not just street cops, but detectives—seemed to derive inordinate pleasure from harassing gays, and people were sick of it.

Most gay historians agree that it was the underlying anger throughout the gay community at being harassed by the police, taunted by thuggish young straights, and treated by society at large as psychopathic "perverts" that made it possible for the Stonewall riots to be enshrined as a symbolic turning point, a revolutionary "moment" that could be celebrated and built upon. The same feelings existed in the big cities across the country, and even gays who didn't know about the Stonewall riots, in San Francisco and Los Angeles, were beginning to stir things up, attempting to take control of their own destinies in new ways. Stonewall became a symbol right off the bat in New York, celebrated a year later with the first Gay Pride Parade. But an explosion had been inevitable. The affirmation of gay life that became the Gay Rights Movement would have taken place even if there had been no riot outside the Stonewall Inn.

It has been 30 years since Stonewall, and as we enter a new century, life has changed dramatically for gays and lesbians. Some of us, mostly in the arts, were out of the closet even in 1969, but millions more have come out in the intervening years. Police officers—men and women—march in gay pride parades now, as do the parents of gays. Local and state politicians in both the Democratic and Republican parties increasingly seek the endorsement of gay organizations, and at the national level both Vice President Gore and former senator Bill Bradley vied for our votes in the fight for the Democratic nomination for president in 2000. Openly gay politicians serve in the House of

Representatives and in half the state legislatures. Laws have been passed in cities large and small across the country to protect us from discrimination in employment and housing. Major corporations, including the family-oriented entertainment giant Disney, have extended health coverage to same-sex partners. Judges in a few states have begun to rule that laws preventing gay adoptions and gay marriages are unconstitutional. For those of us who were adults when the Stonewall riots took place, the world seems a very different and much more livable place. And yet. . . .

We have lived through a time of plague that took the lives of tens of thousands of gay men every year for a decade and that continues to do so at reduced but still horrifying rates. The new laws that protect us from discrimination are still under attack in many parts of the country, and have never been passed in others. In the Republican Party in particular, there are a dozen candidates who seek votes by opposing the gay agenda for every big-city mayor who courts our support. The Republican majority leader of the United States Senate, Trent Lott, declared in 1998 that homosexuals should be classed with alcoholics and kleptomaniacs, and the leading candidate for the Republican presidential nomination in 2000, Governor George W. Bush of Texas, refused to meet with the very staid members of the Log Cabin Republicans, the party's one gay organization. The reason for that antipathy is even more disheartening: the Religious Right, a crucial element of the Republican base vote, unremittingly tries to demonize gays and lesbians as sinners whose sexual orientation is an affront to God. Some go further. When the Vermont Supreme Court declared laws preventing same-sex marriages unconstitutional in December of 1999, another Republican presidential candidate, Gary Bauer, the founder of the Family Research Council, termed it a "terrorist act." Bauer speaks, unfortunately, for millions of fellow Americans who hate and fear us still.

We have made enormous progress since Stonewall, but we still have a long way to go. To win our full place in society as respected citizens with not only the same rights and protections as the heterosexual majority, but also genuine acknowledgement that our sexual orientation has nothing to do with our value as human beings, we will have to continue our battle long into the twenty first century. Yet there is a catch here. Some readers will have noticed it already. I wrote above: " . . . genuine acknowledgement that our sexual orientation has nothing to do with our value as human beings." But that it is only one point of view within the gay community itself. There are many gays who would protest that our sexual orientation has everything to with who we are, that it is crucial to our identity, and that we should value ourselves for our differences instead of trying to persuade the heterosexual majority that we're really just like them. From this point of view, such aspects of the gay rights agenda as gay marriage and gay adoption are ludicrous, and fighting for such "rights" will simply result in poisoning ourselves with heterosexual banalities, or strait-jacketing ourselves with phony conventions.

This split within the gay community between what I call the separatists and the mainstreamers has existed for decades. It was evident even in the largely closeted days before Stonewall, when there were always a few flamboyant gays who didn't give a damn what anybody thought, and it would lead to open warfare within the Gay Rights Movement that developed in the years following Stonewall. I do not mean the terms "separatist" and "mainstreamer" to be taken too literally, however. Within the black Civil Rights Movement there were those who called for literal separatism, with certain states being ceded to African-Americans as all-black enclaves. That kind of programmatic separation has never been a serious aim of even the most radical gays, although primarily gay enclaves have come into existence in major cities on a smaller scale—such as the Castro Street area of San Francisco, and parts of Greenwich Village and Chelsea in New York.

Gay separatists and gay mainstreamers do, however, differ in philosophy, tactics, and general psychology. While gay separatists are fewer in number, they often make up for that by being particularly vocal, given to polemics, and are often confrontational in their tactics. Advocates of gay mainstreaming seek, on the other hand, to downplay differences between gays and straights, using persuasion to work within the largely heterosexual political and legal structure to gain acceptance as productive citizens more like the straight majority than different from it. Both groups want full legal parity with straights, but mainstreamers would say, "The only real difference between us is what we do in bed, and what you do and what we do are both within the limits of normal human behavior." Gay separatists say, "What we do with our bodies is just as valid as what you do, and since there is no such thing as normality, we demand the right to satisfy ourselves according to our standards rather that yours."

At the extremes of the spectrum, we find at one end gay couples who want to get legally married, adopt children, and move to the suburbs to raise them in the midst of straight families that are similarly constituted, while at the other end we find single gay men who want the baths to function as they did before the AIDS crisis, making it possible to have private sex in this public space with as many different partners as their sex drives can sustain. It is certainly possible for both these visions of personal fulfillment to exist simultaneously, but neither group has much interest in promoting one another's aims, and both worry that the other's agenda will interfere with their own. What both groups share is the resistance of the heterosexual majority to the achievement of any gay agenda.

What perhaps needs to be recognized more fully by gay activists in both groups is that there are a great many gays and lesbians who do not whole-heartedly agree with either the separatists or the mainstreamers on many issues. These "third-way" members of the gay community can often sympathize with the arguments and aims of both separatists and mainstreamers to some degree, but also tend to see the problems inherent in the positions on either side. Many third-way members of the gay community, for example, support the idea that gays and lesbians should have the legal right to be married, but would not take advantage of the opportunity if it existed. Some also believe that their sexual nature does make them different from heterosexuals in fundamental ways—and are proud of their "gay sensibility"—yet are still able to enjoy rewarding relationships with straight friends in a way that gay separatists may scorn.

Third-way gays often get short shrift in books about gay history and gay issues. I interviewed many such individuals for my 1980 book *Straight Women/Gay Men: A Special Relationship,* and Edmund White gave them their due in *States of Desire,* also published in 1980. But this large segment of the gay community has often been ignored in recent years. In preparing this book, I once again specifically sought out third-way gays and lesbians to interview, although I also talked to some adamant separatists and numerous mainstreamers. The comments from third-way gays and lesbians that you will find throughout this new book help to put the views of gay activists—both separatists and mainstreamers—into perspective, and may in some cases provide a kind of bridge between divergent views on many issues crucial to the gay community as we enter a new century.

In the chapters that follow, I will be dealing with seven areas of major concern to the gay community: AIDS; coming out, gay marriage, gay adoption, gays and politics, gays and religion, and violence against gays. In the final chapter I will be taking a broader look at how the history and current status of these issues may ultimately affect gay life over the next two decades. In each of the seven chapters on specific subjects, I will be looking back at the historical events that shaped these issues both within the gay community and the larger society we live in; chronicling recent legal, political, and social developments that illustrate where things stand at present; and quoting extensively from both gay leaders and the gays and lesbians I interviewed about where we should be headed.

The gay community is unquestionably more diverse than the general public fully understands, yet even some gay leaders do not always seem to fully recognize how multifaceted it is. That very diversity gives rise to tension within the community itself, and when those tensions flare into public acrimony between gay leaders, the general public sometimes becomes further confused. Worse, name-calling between gay leaders and writers too often gives aid and comfort to our worst enemies. The Religious Right has proved itself all too adept at exploiting dissension in the gay community and playing up extreme statements or actions. At the same time, however, the anti-gay forces in our society often resort to such extremes that they only further motivate gays and lesbians—and discredit themselves with the enormous American political and social center.

All this pushing and pulling creates an inevitable seesaw effect that cuts both for and against the achievement of gay civil rights. When a court rules—as has now happened in both Hawaii and Vermont—that laws against same-sex marriages are unconstitutional, the symbolic gains for gays can be offset by frantic efforts by well-organized anti-gay groups to pull the rug out from beneath gay progress through voter referendums, state legislation and even Congress. That attack further galvanizes gays and lesbians to fight back. Meanwhile, the general public watches from the sidelines, with one event gaining some additional sympathy for gays, another creating a degree of backlash. As the stakes increase, disagreements on tactics and positions resurface with a sometimes unfortunate clangor within the gay community, as a long-established battle between the fear of backlash on the one hand, and the fear of complacency on the other, plays itself out all over again.

Do loud arguments within the gay community seriously damage future prospects for success? Or do they demonstrate a diversity that is one of our strengths? While the efforts of moderate gays to bring about change incrementally through quiet dealings with the political establishment sometimes reap considerable rewards, do we not still sometimes have the need of the confrontational tactics of gay radicals? Is it possible for both gay separatists and gay mainstreamers to get what they want down the line, or are their philosophies and aims antithetical? What role can, or should, the less vocal third-way gays play in mediating disagreements between gay separatists and gay mainstreamers?

These are some of the questions that will be examined here. You will encounter a broad spectrum of answers to them. I have made every effort to give a balanced account of the differences that exist within the gay community, and to avoid taking sides. No doubt some of my personal biases will show through from time to time, but I believe that most readers will find that what may appear to be a degree of bias in one context will get turned around in another. The only group I will be treating with deserved antipathy are the anti-gay zealots on the Religious Right. They are sworn enemies of all gays and lesbians, and I am more than happy to give them a hard time. And please keep in mind that although I will report the disdain that some gay leaders hold for others, because it is essential to the story, that does not necessarily mean that I agree with it. Gay leaders and writers will find in these page both the praise and the brickbats that they are all too familiar with—but at least they will find both.

Two points about the writing of this book still need to be made. The first concerns the identities of the dozens of individuals I interviewed for this book. Almost all of them are out of the closet, but to varying degrees. This is a touchy subject that I deal with at length in chapter 3, on "coming out." But almost everyone I interviewed asked to be identified by their first names only, even the considerable number who are completely out. Their reason for requesting such semi-anonymity usually had to do with basic matters of personal privacy rather than the fact that they are gay or lesbian. They did not want to have the local newspapers calling them up for quotes on gay issues, or to find themselves the object of abusive e-mail. They did not want to put themselves in the position of being gay spokespersons; some who spoke with particular frankness were more concerned about alienating friends than they were about the reactions of straight friends or co-workers. As one lesbian in her thirties put it, "I have straight friends who married what I consider to be jerks, of both sexes, but I certainly didn't tell them to their faces. And I don't want my lesbian friends who are wild about the idea of getting married to know that I think the idea is silly, either." There are also some people I interviewed whose profession, such as that of a junior high school teacher, precludes public identification as a gay man or lesbian.

Secondly, there is the matter of written sources. The bibliography contains a list of more than fifty books that are either named in the text or that proved valuable in terms of research. There are dozens of others, read over the past forty-odd years, that have informed and enlightened me that are not recorded here. I followed the coverage of gay issues in a number of major newspapers and national magazines, and many people sent me clippings from local papers across the country. These are mentioned only when I have directly quoted them or drawn information from them. The same is true for numerous gay publications, from the pornographic to the slick to the professional journal or newsletter.

I have made considerable use of articles from the *New York Times,* and there is deep irony in that fact. There are many gays who have never forgiven the *Times* for its treatment of gays and gay issues during the long period during which Abe Rosenthal was the executive editor of the paper; he would not even allow the word gay to be used in the paper unless it was part of a title, like "Gay Men's Chorus." He also got a reputation as being personally homophobic. Walter Clemons, the well-known book critic for *Newsweek,* who died in 1996 from the complications of a lifelong struggle with diabetes, was very certain that that he has been denied the post of daily critic for the *Times* because Rosenthal did not want a gay man in the job. This story was told in Charles Kaiser's book *Gay Metropolis,* but I would like to attest to its veracity. I met Walter when he was living in Rome in 1963, and he became a steadfast friend. He was also my landlord for several years, renting me and my lover Paul Baldwin our first apartment, in his house in Long Island City in 1970. Walter was very angry about being denied the job at the *Times,* and told me what happened in detail—although in the end he would admit he was probably better off at *Newsweek,* where he got to write numerous cover stories in the arts.

But the *Times* began using the word gay as soon as Abe Rosenthal retired from his post, and in the last several years it has become the leader among mainstream publications in covering gay issues and events, particularly in regard to legal developments and the struggle over gay rights within American religious denominations. These days, gay issues are the subject of almost daily articles in the *Times*, sometimes several on one day, and it was an invaluable resource in writing this book. The change that has taken place at the *Times* is symbolic of the vastly greater acceptance of homosexuals in our society that has developed in the years since Stonewall. But even now, many of the stories that appear in the paper are about the difficulties we still face in achieving our rightful places in American society. There is still deep prejudice to combat and bigots in high places who seek to deny us not only our legal rights but our very sense of self-worth. The rights to marry, adopt children, or serve openly in the military have now become unfinished business in a new century. This book is about where we are now, how we got here, and how our story may play out in the challenging years directly ahead.

two

AIDS: Past, Present, and Future

The first indication that something was wrong came in the May 18, 1981, issue of *The New York Native,* the small but feisty gay newspaper that specialized in covering gay politics in New York. The article was written by Larry Mass, a gay M.D., and dealt with the rumors that gays were getting unaccountably ill with a rare form of pneumonia. The New York Health Department listed eleven such cases, one of which had resulted in death. The editors of the newspaper gave the article the reassuring headline DISEASE RUMORS LARGELY UNFOUNDED, which was in contradiction to its content.

The Centers for Disease Control, the federal health agency in Atlanta charged with the prevention and control of communicable disease, noted in its weekly newsletter during the first week of July that twenty homosexual men in New York City and six in California had been diagnosed with a rare form of cancer known as Karposi's sarcoma, which resulted in skin lesions. The *New York Times* picked up on that story, and using its own research upped the number afflicted with this cancer to forty-one. It was the *Times* story that really started people talking in the gay community—somewhat ironically, considering the institutional homophobia at the *Times* during that period.

The disease that was attacking homosexual men was first called GRID, for gay-related immune deficiency, a name that, it was quickly realized, stigmatized gays, and the term AIDS, for acquired immune deficiency syndrome, was soon given the imprimatur of the Centers for Disease Control. The story of the ensuing AIDS crisis has been told in dozens of books, ranging from Randy Shilts' bestselling *And the Band Played On*,_which won National Book Critics Circle Award for 1987, to such personal accounts as Paul Monette's wrenching *On Borrowed Time* of 1988 and Fenton Johnson's moving 1996 memoir *Geography of the Heart*. The AIDS story—which escalated from a few rumors to a worldwide health crisis in a mere three years, and from a gay-related panic to a public-health emergency that knows no borders and has become a heterosexual menace in countries around the world—does not need retelling in detail here. But several aspects of it have a specific bearing on how the Gay Rights Movement may be expected to fare in the 21st century in the United States.

AIDS hit the American gay community at a time when there was a tendency toward complacency. There had been a scary time in 1977 and 1978, during which gays and lesbians had to marshal all their energy to combat the anti-gay crusade of Save the Children, Inc., founded by singing orange juice promoter Anita Bryant. She and her cronies initially succeeded in overturning a gay rights ordinance in Dade County, Florida. Bryant had singled out gay teachers as a danger to American children, but she went too far. Met by gay protestors at every stop, her ever-ready tears initially brought her public sympathy, but she was so extreme in her views that her fervor soon turned her into the butt of media jokes. The Bryant-inspired Proposition 6, also known as the Briggs Amendement, was defeated in California in 1978 when President Ford, Democratic nominee Jimmy Carter, and even former governor Ronald Reagan all came out against it. The murder of San Francisco mayor George Moscone and gay supervisor Harvey Milk by the just-defeated former supervisor Dan White following the 1978 election served to alert the general public to be wary of anti-gay extremists. In the next two and a half years there were political or legal successes in some cities and defeats in others, but much of the gay community wasn't paying real attention. They were too busy having a good time.

At the start of the 1980s, the loudest voices in the gay community were proclaiming that the real meaning of gay liberation was recreational sex and lots of it. The bathhouses in New York and San Francisco had taken on the guise of a perpetual orgy. Bars with darkened back rooms where sex continued until dawn were flourishing as never before, ignored by police. For the more timid, there were gay movie houses showing the latest porn film; there you could spot businessmen in pin-striped suits masturbating at three in the afternoon. The day would come when such men would be glad they weren't habitues of the baths.

There were of course many gay men who weren't to be found in the baths, or the movie houses, or the public toilets, although they might have checked them out at one time or another. There were plenty of men who had settled partners, or who were looking for them in the more sedate bars with no back rooms. Lesbians looked on the baths largely with disdain, and gay activist groups were often in a state of flux or riven with internal conflict because of the differences between those who thought that gay liberation was about protective legislation and those who thought it was about sex.

Once the full dimensions of the AIDS epidemic began to become clear, in 1982 and 1983, the hedonistic gays had a very difficult time coming to terms with what was happening to them. In New York and San Francisco there was fierce resistance to closing the baths and back-room bars. Some gays were even outraged at the idea of posting notices warning about the dangers of AIDS. I ran into a Harvard classmate outside Bloomingdales in New York one day. He was a soap opera actor, with that kind of flashy handsomeness typical of the breed, and he was in a rage about rumors that Mayor Ed Koch was going to close the bars. Although he spoke in a low voice, with people passing us on the sidewalk, his intensity was ferocious. Not only did he feel the city had no right to close the baths, but he took the very idea personally. "I am 43," he said, with fury in his eyes, "and I haven't got much time left." What he meant, of course, was that in spite of his buffed body and the plastic surgery he'd recently had around his eyes, he was getting almost too old to be wanted by the younger men who attracted him. But he spoke more truth than he knew, or perhaps wanted to know. In two years, he would be dead from AIDS.

The controversy over the baths was bad enough in New York. In San Francisco, it became almost fratricidal. An attempt in 1984 by the popular director of the Department of Public Health, Mervyn Silverman, to enlist the support of gay leaders in endorsing the closing of the bathhouses ended in disaster, as some who had agreed to sign a statement backed off because the anger among the bathhouse supporters became so intense. On April 4, 1984, an editorial in the gay paper the *Bay Area Reporter* by Paul Lorch attacked by name 16 gay men and lesbians who had been involved in this attempt to close the bathhouses. As reported in *And the Band Played On,* Lorch called these gay leaders "collaborators," writing, "These 16 people would have killed the movement, glibly handing it over to the forces that have beaten us down since time immemorial. . . ." This "traitors list" included gay supervisor Harry Britt, who had succeeded Harvey Milk; Dick Pabich, who had been the first to discover Milk's murdered body; and Frank Robinson, the science fiction writer who had penned Harvey Milk's campaign speeches, championing gay liberation with uncommon eloquence. As Randy Shilts pointed out, the sixteen traitors comprised an honors list of San Francisco political gay leaders—who were now suddenly the enemy.

For those who insisted that gay liberation and recreational sex were inextricably intertwined, AIDS was seen simply as an excuse on the part of the heterosexual majority to take away a freedom that had been far too long in arriving. At the start of the AIDS crisis, such gays insisted that there was no proof that AIDS was spread by sexual contact because the virus itself had not been identified; besides, a vaccine would quickly be found, bringing the epidemic to an end in short order. Even when the virus was identified, almost simultaneously, in France and the United States in April of 1984, the defenders of the bathhouses would not bend, mustering outrage at even the suggestion that safe sex ought to be practiced. In San Francisco they fought a legal battle to keep the bathhouses open, but in the end they closed down for the lack of business—people were too frightened to go to them. By December of 1985, even New York's famous New St. Marks Baths had closed its doors.

The intransigence of the bathhouse defenders was a major political setback for the gay community as a whole. The Religious Right used AIDS as a battering ram against gay liberation early on. The Rev. Jerry Falwell made headlines when he spoke at a Moral Majority rally on July 4, 1983, by intoning that AIDS was a "judgement of God" on homosexuals, and calling the disease "the plague of the century." This speech, hardly unexpected, was extreme enough to disturb neutral observers, and some editorials and commentary took Falwell to task for presuming to know God's will. And calling AIDS the plague of the century at that point was blatant exaggeration; it would be another 10 months before the number of known cases even reached four thousand. Falwell was managing to forget the Spanish flu epidemic of 1918–1919, which had killed more than 21 million victims worldwide. But as the number of cases continued to mount, at first slowly, then alarmingly, Falwell began to look like a prophet, to the great dismay of the gay community. Even worse for gay rights politics, mainstream publications and commentators who had been sympathetic to the movement began to criticize the bathhouse intransigents for putting their own selfish sexual interests ahead of the medical well-being of the general population.

Gay leaders found themselves in a crossfire between the militants who equated liberation with recreational sex, and a general backlash against what now seemed like dangerous homosexual practices. Why couldn't sensible, responsible gays—many wanted to know—control the hedonistic militants among them? The truth was that the gay rights movement had never been monolithic. The majority might simply want to be allowed to live their lives in peace, with basic legal protection against discrimination. But it was militants who had gotten the gay liberation movement rolling, at Stonewall and in the years immediately following it. So many gays and lesbians had been and remained closeted, allowing more courageous and often more flamboyant figures to lead the movement, that they had little power to control the militants now. Even within the cadre of leaders there had long been bitter debates about tactics, with a new group of activists who knew how to work the political system from the inside often at odds with those who wanted to use more aggressive forms of protest. The gay separatists and the gay mainstreamers too often ended up at one another's throats. But a great many gays understood that both kind of leaders were necessary. That was especially true of closeted gays who gave money to gay causes, but were in no way public activists.

Bob, now a white-haired seventy-four-year-old, remembers it all, including the painful days when AIDS struck and he found himself in the middle of a ferocious debate between two of his closest friends, both former lovers. "I was in the closet, mostly, until I retired. Thought I had to be, the old story. But I loved the baths. Fortunately I wasn't into anal sex, top or bottom, or I probably would have been dead long ago. I was blessed with a very beautiful dick, so I was always able to do just fine at the baths, even in my fifties. Over the years, I have had several love affairs, but I was between regular partners in the early 1980s. I stopped going to the baths by February of 1982, just around the time the Gay Men's Health Crisis was formed. One of my former lovers, Larry, got involved with that. He wasn't a founder, but he believed in what they were doing—helping gay men cops with AIDS. Another former lover was completely on the other side. His name was Jock—really, that's what everyone called him from high school, when he started wearing jockstraps instead of underwear. Jock was wild and insatiable. 'I come more often than I pee,' he used to say, and it was true. Peed four times a day, ejaculated five."

Bob shakes his head. "I couldn't begin to keep up with Jock. Few could. He and Larry knew one another well, got it on occasionally for a while. They were both younger than I was, Larry was in his early forties, and Jock about thirty-four when AIDS struck. For Jock, the baths *were* gay liberation. That was the *raison d'etre.* There were a lot like him in that regard. Larry was much more serious, more politically inclined, thought anti-discrimination laws were the object, not just the freedom to get it off with strangers every few hours. AIDS set them against one another. It really blew up when two young guys who were already sick published an article in the *New York Native* at the end of 1982. Berkowwitz, one was called, but I've forgotten the other name. I didn't know them, but Jock did. He absolutely exploded over the article. The article was headed WE KNOW WHO WE ARE, I recall, and had something about declaring war on promiscuity. To Jock they were traitors, to Larry they were brave men facing up to the disaster that their promiscuity had brought on themselves and others. Jock and Larry had it out at a small dinner party at my apartment, screaming at the top of their lungs while the rest of us sat there in shock. We intervened when Jock started swinging at Larry. Jock never spoke to Larry or me again. Amazingly, Jock didn't get AIDS until 1985, one of those crazy exceptions. He wouldn't accept help from anyone. Went down to a cabin in the woods in the Poconos and shot himself when he realized it was hopeless. Larry never did get it. He'd gone to the baths too, but in that kind of situation he was a watcher. He died just last year, of a heart attack. But I'll never forget that evening at my apartment when the two of them went at each other. What have we come to, I thought. This is as bad as the disease itself."

The two young gay men who wrote the article accepting a degree of blame for the spread of AIDS were Richard Berkowitz and Michael Callen. They had been influenced by the attitudes and writings of Larry Kramer, who to this day is a major voice in the gay community and still capable of causing an uproar. Kramer had been nominated for an Oscar for his screenplay for Ken Russell's 1970 movie *Women in Love,* from a D. H. Lawrence novel that had long been regarded as unfilmable. In 1978 he published a novel, *Faggots,* which gave a far grittier and more realistic view of the gay sexual underground than anyone had previously attempted. Kramer would say that he intended the book to be funny, but it repulsed many mainstream critics and enraged many gays, including such prominent figures as gay historian Martin

Duberman, author of *Stonewall,* who attacked it scathingly in *The New Republic.*

Kramer was one of the first among prominent gays to recognize the potential scope of the AIDS epidemic, and convened a meeting of eighty gay men in his New York apartment in August of 1981 to hear what Dr. Alvin Freidman-Kein had to say about the new disease. Freidman-Kein, a dermatologist attached to the New York University Medical Center, had been the first physician to identify cases of Kaposi's sarcoma in gay men in the city. That meeting would lead to the formation of the Gay Men's Health Crisis (GMHC) in January 1982 at Kramer's apartment at 1 Fifth Avenue, overlooking Washington Square. Kramer was elected to the board, but a very handsome and personable businessman named Paul Popham was chosen president despite the fact that he had previously been semi-closeted and never taken part in gay politics. It is widely agreed by commentators on this period that Kramer was too controversial for the position of president, since he was detested by many of the well-heeled gay men from whom the GMHC hoped to raise money. Indeed, Kramer would prove too controversial even for the organization itself within fifteen months.

This early period of the AIDS crisis was one of confusion and denial for the majority of gays. There were gay men fighting to keep the baths open, there were others trying to get city governments to provide funds to care for the increasing number of men who were ill or dying, there were gays trying to ignore the entire problem, hoping it would soon go away. The mainstream press was ignoring the issue, politicians were either turning a deaf ear—as was the case with Mayor Ed Koch of New York—or finding themselves almost paralyzed by conflicting political needs, as was the case with Mayor Diane Feinstein of San Francisco. The unmarried Koch, whom many gays and a few heterosexuals suspected of being a closeted homosexual, didn't want to get involved. Feinstein felt something had to be done about the baths, but was trying not to offend her many gay supporters. Some specialists in the medical community were becoming increasingly alarmed, certain that if gay men did not abstain from sex or take stringent precautions, the disease would spread like wildfire; but the medical profession as a whole didn't want to even think about the problem.

At times the situation bordered on the comic, as when Paul Popham and Larry Kramer got into an argument—later reported by Randy Shilts—because Popham was worried that the word "gay" in the name of the GMHC would alert his mailman and doorman to the fact that he was homosexual. Kramer suggested that his doorman might have already figured that out since Popham often took tricks back to his apartment late at night. It had been nearly thirteen years since Stonewall, and the gay community, at least in the large cities, had at least achieved the objective of being let alone by the police. But it was becoming clearer by the day that the Gay Rights Movement still had not grown up.

Into this murk, Kramer launched an explosive article that would finally begin to light up the troubled landscape in a way that could not be ignored. Called 1,112 AND COUNTING, in reference to the current number of known AIDS cases, the article was published by the *New York Native* in its mid-March issue in the spring of 1983. The first sentence of the piece read. "If this article doesn't scare the shit out of you, we're in real trouble." It went on to conclude that "Unless we fight for our lives, we shall die. In the history of homosexuality we have never been so close to death and extinction before." Those in denial were furious with Kramer all over again for what was seen as his anti-sex position. But the article was reprinted in gay publications across the country and both the gay community and the mainstream press began to pay a new kind of attention to AIDS. Three weeks later, *Newsweek* put the mysterious epidemic on its cover, and AIDS finally became a national concern. In the next three months, Randy Shilts would later note, there were 680 stories on AIDS, seventeen times the number that had appeared in the last three months of 1982. Ironically, Kramer's bombshell also led to his severing his ties with the GMHC. Left out as a delegate to a long-sought meeting with Mayor Koch on April 14, Kramer resigned from the board of directors of the organization he had been instrumental in founding.

Now a new fight began: to get government funding for AIDS research. It would prove an endlessly frustrating battle, as the conservative administration of President Ronald Reagan steadfastly tried to downplay the epidemic and the need for special funds. The House of Representatives was forcefully and eloquently led on this issue by Representative Henry Waxman of California. Waxman was a staunch liberal whose Los Angeles district included a number of areas where gays and lesbians had settled. As early as April of 1982, Waxman made an opening statement at a hearing on the subject of Kaposi's sarcoma before the Subcommittee on Health and the Environment, which he chaired, that made clear his grasp of both the health threat and the political problems connected with it. "I want to be especially blunt about the political aspects of Kaposi's sarcoma," he said. "This horrible disease afflicts one of the nation's most stigmatized and discriminated against minorities. The victims are not typical Main Street Americans. They are gays, mainly from New York, Los Angeles, and San Francisco. There is no doubt in my mind that, if the same disease had appeared among Americans of Norwegian descent, or among tennis players, rather than among gay males, the responses of both the government and the medical community would have been different."

Over the next four years it would be up to Congress to add AIDS funds to the budget despite the objections of the Reagan administration. It was obvious to the gay community that the president and his wife Nancy had a number of gay friends, but Reagan failed to even acknowledge the existence of the disease in any public statement. It was not until July 25, 1985, when it was announced that Rock Hudson had gone to the Pasteur Institute for treatment of AIDS, that even Reagan began to bend. The word of Hudson's acknowledgement that he had AIDS was headline news around the world, and the White House issued a statement to say that the President had called his longtime friend to wish him well. As numerous writers and commentators have noted, the revelation about Hudson changed everything in terms of public and governmental attitudes toward the disease. There have been few events in the television age that have indicated more clearly the immense impact that major celebrities have on the media that cashes in on their stories and the general public that follows their every move.

While the gay community was happy and relieved that the Hudson story altered public perception of the AIDS crisis, it was common to hear gay men say, "Where was all this sympathy when my lover died?" There were also many charges that innumerable lives could have been saved if the virus had been isolated sooner. Such accusations were sometimes answered by saying that the gay community itself had been in denial about the seriousness of the epidemic. But, the retort came back, if the virus had been identified in 1982 instead of 1984, and work had begun to combat it, gays would have grasped extreme danger of unsafe sex much sooner, and tens of thousands might not have been affected at all, while those who were might have had years added to their lives with the drugs that eventually became available. The end result of the foot-dragging that took place on both sides was an epidemic that was almost out of control before serious steps were taken to deal with it.

Even after the HTLV-III virus had been identified as the cause of AIDS, full mobilization against the disease took time. AIDS researchers were distracted by the acrimonious debate between the American team headed by Dr. Robert Gallo and the French team at the Pasteur Institute headed by Dr. Luc Montagnier about which had been the first to discover the virus. Nobel prizes might be at stake, but all the gay community now cared about was that progress be made in controlling the disease. And where was the money to help care for the thousands already affected, whose numbers were increasing daily?

In April of 1985, Larry Kramer once again stepped forward to give additional impetus to the battle against AIDS. The opening of his play about AIDS, *The Normal Heart,* gave a new focus to the story. While many New York gay leaders had heard some of the speeches in the play from Kramer's own mouth to the point that they were sick of hearing the words, he had packaged his own outrage in a piece of political theater that left some critics weeping, brought rave reviews from major publications, and made tickets to the performances at Joseph Papp's Public Theater the hottest ones in town. But this was more than just a theatrical success. Copies of the script were circulated around the city, and Mayor Koch, who was attacked by name in the play, announced an expansion of city services for AIDS patients hours before the first preview. Kramer had gotten the gay community to take AIDS with fresh seriousness two years earlier with his article in the *New York Native.* Now he had prodded the government of the great city with the largest number of AIDS victims into fresh action. And he had done it with a play that also made heterosexuals realize once again that the fundamental meaning of gay liberation was tied up with human liberty and not just sexual license.

Two years later, Kramer unleashed another of his patented diatribes at the founding meeting of a new organization, the AIDS Coalition to Unleash Power (ACT-UP), which took place in New York on March 10, 1987. Fueled by rising anger about not only the lack of sufficient funds to battle AIDS at all levels of government, and the exorbitant price and slow release of AIDS drugs, but also the demonization of gays in the media and among the general public, ACT-UP members made their outrage known in public demonstrations that created headlines. Its activities had more in common with the Stonewall riots than with the patient-oriented activities of the GMHC, which Kramer had the vengeful pleasure of denouncing as a bunch of "nurse's aides." In attacking the group he had helped to found, he understood exactly how the pun on AIDS would sting.

ACT-UP, with demonstrations on Wall Street, at the headquarters of the Food and Drug Administration in Washington, and in front of the White House (where the demonstrators were arrested by police wearing yellow gloves to protect them from the supposed danger of contamination), made it clear that gays were mad as hell and were not going to take it anymore, to use the cry from the movie *Network* of eleven years earlier—back then, gays had been willing to scream about what was being done to them. With ACT-UP, they started to make real noise again. The radicals were in the vanguard of the gay rights movement once more, and they were badly needed.

Yet even as the medical and political drama of the AIDS crisis was playing out in the headlines, a quieter and, in the end, far more positive change was taking place. The AIDS crisis was centered in the big cities, particularly the gay meccas of New York, San Francisco, and Los Angeles, where thousands of gay men from lesser cities, small towns and even rural areas had gone to live among others like them. In New

York's Greenwich Village or San Francisco's Castro Street area there were not just bars but restaurants, bookstores, and shops that catered to them, giving them a sense of belonging to a coherent culture instead of being outsiders in a straight middle-class environment. For some gays, working in the theatre or other arts professions, the big cities were a place where they could be completely out of the closet. Others were closeted at work, but at night and on the weekends they could be themselves among their own people. A surprising number were not out with their own families, however; if their parents came to visit, they would have to hide pictures and books in their apartments, take their parents to restaurants they did not usually frequent, and even ask a lover to spend a few days staying with a friend— preferably, in many cases, a lesbian friend. Some parents might ask probing questions and get lied to, while others would pretend to have to no suspicions and some might be genuinely clueless about the kind of life their son really lived. But AIDS changed the scenario. Hundreds, and eventually thousands of young men, and some who were in their forties and fifties, became ill. Once AZT, the first drug treatment to affect the life cycle of the AIDS virus and thus prolong lives, was introduced in 1986, it was possible to hide the truth a while longer. But in the end thousands of young men would have to tell their families that they had AIDS and that they were going to die, and in towns across the country there were parents, sometimes bewildered, sometimes angry, who had to come to terms with the fact that their beloved son was "a fairy," "queer," "a faggot," and that the kind of sex that gave him joy was now going to kill him. And, despite profound dismay, or anger, or shame, a great many parents said, "Come home, son, we'll take care of you."

Ada, the mother of a friend of mine who died of AIDS, remembers vividly what it was like. "My husband Ben and I have lived our entire lives in a small town in Iowa. Ben was a lawyer and I was a school teacher. For our own town, we were relatively sophisticated people, I suppose, although Iowa has a great educational system and most people know what's going on in the world. We had two children, our daughter Rachel and Mike. Mike had a golden voice even as a child, and we weren't surprised when he decided to go to the University of

Indiana, which had a wonderful music department, and then to New York after college to try to break into show business."

It was after Mike came to New York that I got to know him. He was in several shows in summer theater that starred my lover Paul Baldwin, including *Man of La Mancha* and *Sweeny Todd*. Mike had a beautiful tenor voice and an angelic face that belied a wicked sense of humor. He became a good friend of mine as well as Paul's, and we saw a lot of him and his lover, Jim, who was in the record business. Mike and Jim were younger than we were and lived a somewhat wilder life. Even so, it was not until 1990 that they were found to be HIV-positive. In spite of AZT, Jim was gone in just over a year; Mike lasted two years, the last ten months spent in Iowa with his parents.

"Mike never told us he was gay, and I guess we just tried to ignore what we knew had to be true. He told his sister, but she was married and living in Oregon and she never brought it up with us. Ben and I didn't discuss it, and we didn't see much of Mike, although he called every week. When he was in college we drove to Indiana to see him perform several times, but we only saw him in a professional show once, in a theater in Ohio. He sent us audio tapes of all his shows, though, and a couple of times the shows were videotaped, and he sent us those. We shared them all with our friends. We were very proud of him. But although we had met Jim once—he came out to Ohio at the same time we were there—and often talked to him on the phone, we had no real idea about their life together. Jim seemed very nice and sensible, and we thought he was probably a steadying influence on Mike, who could be a little irresponsible, especially about money. I remember asking Mike after he came home with AIDS if he'd gotten it from Jim; since Jim had died first, it made sense that he'd been infected first. But Mike said that didn't mean anything, how long you lived didn't necessarily have anything to do with when you were exposed. He said they had no idea who had been infected first, since they were diagnosed as being HIV-positive within days of one another. Then he said, "We liked three-way sex, Mom, it probably happened at the same time." That shocked me so much I couldn't even cry. That was stupid of me, I came to realize, but I had led a very sheltered existence in many ways."

"When Mike came home, he was already quite sick, and things got worse for him quickly. Both Ben and I were angry, with him, with Jim, with ourselves. We tried not to show it. Mike was so sick and he tried so hard to be cheerful. We couldn't take it out on him. And we had to ask ourselves if we were angry in part because his having AIDS was so difficult for us in our town. There were a couple of 'old bachelors' in town, but nobody ever thought of them in terms of sex. They did travel more than most people. And I assumed they behaved differently when they did, but at home they were just sweet old eccentrics. Of course they were young once, and I think now they must have been lovers in their youth, maybe always, although they didn't live together and gave the impression they merely tolerated each other. One of them lived out on a country road, so they might have spent a great deal of time together without anyone paying much attention."

"But when Mike came home, everybody paid attention. We told our minister about what was going on before Mike arrived. He was very sympathetic, and toward Mike as well as us, but he gave us bad advice. He told us to say Mike had cancer and let it go at that. But he didn't have cancer, jut endless bouts of pneumonia, which hardly makes sense in Iowa in July and August. People kept asking questions, dripping with concern, but really quite nosy and aggressive. After he'd been home two months, and hospitalized twice, Mike said that if we didn't tell people he was going to stand in the middle of the town by the soldiers' memorial and start screaming, 'I have AIDS,' over and over again, so we told a few close friends. They said things like, 'We were afraid it might be that.' No, THAT, as though it was capitalized like AIDS, which they couldn't quite manage. Of course, it was all over town in twenty-four hours, and people would come up to us and say, 'Are you managing all right,' peering at us as though we might break out in boils at any second. There were people who wouldn't shake hands with Ben anymore, and women wouldn't touch me, and we got tired of being treated like lepers. We got mad ourselves. So Ben and I sat down and wrote a long letter, with every hard fact we could find about AIDS. We sent it to a local newspaper, which came out once a week. It turned out the editor had a cousin with AIDS, out in California, and he was more than willing to publish our letter. He said he'd even write an editorial. But he wanted to be sure we realized what we might be getting into. Mike had read the letter and just sobbed, saying how sorry he was about messing up our lives. And we both held him, and said it didn't matter, and he just rocked back and forth in our arms for ten minutes, crying.

"The letter was published, and the editorial to go with it. When the paper was printed, Mike said to us, 'My God, you've become gay rights activists!' And we said we guessed that was right. Well, there were a couple of people who wouldn't speak to us after that, including a woman from our own church, but most people said they'd learned a lot. It was much easier after that. By taking a stand for Mike we changed ourselves, and I think we changed our town, too. It took a while, but attitudes shifted. And when Mike died, so many people came to the funeral that they couldn't all get into the church. So the minister rigged up some speakers for the people outside. And the last thing before the final prayer, we played a tape Mike had sent us ten years earlier of him singing 'The Only Home I Know,' from the musical *Shenandoah*. It's a song sung by a wounded soldier at the end of the Civil War, and it was perfect for Mike's tenor voice. He sounded like an angel on high, and I have never heard so many people crying at a funeral."

Rock Hudson's death from AIDS provided the initial shock that caused the general public to begin shifting its attitudes toward the disease, but it was parents like Ada and Ben who carried the flag in subsequent years, as more and more sons returned home to die and their parents took courageous steps to educate themselves and their communities about not only AIDS but homosexuality itself. They wrote letters to local newspapers, and formed committees, and marched in gay pride parades with their sons and daughters. The cost of human lives was exorbitantly high, but the AIDS crisis was not without its beneficial effects for the Gay Rights Movement. While AIDS initially hardened public views against homosexuality, the ever-rising death toll eventually had the opposite effect. The sheer numerical count of the dead and dying forced many people to recognize that there were far more gay men in the world than they allowed themselves to see, often men they knew and respected, even cherished, men who had been closeted but who were now forced out into the open because of their illness. Friends from college, co-workers, brothers and nephews, and more than a few men who were godfathers to the children of friends were now victims of an incurable plague. "Well, if my dear friends Billy and Sam are gay, and dying from a sexually transmitted disease," many heterosexuals found themselves saying, "I guess I'd better start rethinking what I feel about homosexuals."

Within the gay community itself, however, it was difficult to accept that any such beneficial changes were evolving—too many tragic deaths were occurring, too many close friends and former, or current, lovers were dying agonizing deaths. Paul and I lost many friends to AIDS, although there were others who went through far more grief. To some, the toll seemed insupportable. One woman we know, a professional actress who was herself a lesbian, attended more than one hundred funerals between 1982 and 1998 in New York City. Paul and I more often heard about the deaths of friends from letters or phone calls, since we moved to Florida to be with my eighty-eight-year old father in 1986, and remained with him until his death from a stroke in 1992. But we got the *New York Times* every day, and it was often full of bad news about AIDS deaths. One day in 1989, a story about a friend was on the front page. Tom Wirth was not an important person, just an exceptionally nice one, and ordinarily neither his life nor his death would have drawn the attention of the *Times.* But there he was, because of AIDS.

I had met Tom in December of 1963, when I was back in New York for a few months after living in Europe since 1961. A mutual friend, the writer Dolores Klaich, who would later write the fine book on the lesbian experience *Woman Plus Woman,* invited both Tom and me to her West 11 th Street apartment for dinner, and afterward I went home with him. Tom was just over six feet, slender and very handsome, with black wavy hair and blue eyes. We had a terrific time in bed that snowy night in his apartment on the Bowery, but I returned to Europe a couple of weeks later. We became good friends after my return to New York in November of 1965. Dolores and Tom and I, and a number of other gays and lesbians, with a few straight friends mixed in, saw a lot of one another. I have particularly fond memories of a pot-luck Thanksgiving at his new apartment in the far East Village in 1971. Paul and I were there, and Dolores, and gay friends of Tom's from Boston and Paris, as well as our straight friend Maria, and a number of others. It was an extremely festive occasion, and there were many others like it, with Tom soon including his lover Gene.

These many occasions came flooding back when I read about Tom in the *Times.* I knew that Gene had died of AIDS and that Tom was ill too. Tom was now in a coma and the reason his story was front page news was that gay rights organizations had mobilized to force the courts to allow Tom to be removed from life-support. Gene had suffered prolonged agonies when he was dying, and Tom had signed every possible document to assure that he would be allowed to die peacefully when all hope was gone. But the hospital had ultimately refused to honor his signed requests, which included a living will. Tom's case made Paul and me angry, and we were hardly alone. For in addition to eventually changing attitudes towards homosexuals, the AIDS crisis also had an important effect on the nascent right-to-die movement, with repercussions that are still being felt across the country. And so Tom's final fight, carried out for him by others on the basis of documents he had signed, gave his life and death a new meaning not just in terms of gay rights, but also in the terms of an entirely different social cause that has become as important to many heterosexuals as it is to gays. It was a strange public ending to the life of one of the gentlest and most modest human beings I have ever known.

AIDS changed a great many things, bringing a tragic early end to many splendid lives even as it affected an entire society, and ultimately the world, on numerous levels. It is still changing America and the world, because it is still very much with us. In 1998 the first country-by-country analysis of AIDS infection, carried out by the United

Nations, concluded that 30 million people around the world carried the AIDS virus—21 million of them in Africa, where it is chiefly heterosexuals that are affected. That puts it in the same league as the two greatest medical scourges of human history, the Black Death that began in the Middle Ages and killed 2 million people in India as recently as 1920, and the influenza pandemic of 1918–1919 that started at Fort Riley, Kansas, and took more than 21 million lives before burning itself out. The Black Death still worries international health officials, who believe it could resurface at any time, but AIDS remains an almost overwhelming front-burner health crisis with no end in sight.

The fact that in the rest of the world AIDS has become primarily a heterosexual disease has taken the pressure off the gay community in the United States, at least in terms of public opinion. It s now believed that the AIDS virus made the crucial leap from monkeys or chimpanzees to humans in Africa as long ago as the early 1950s or late 1940s. That means that there would undoubtedly have been an AIDS epidemic regardless of the promiscuous sex that gays practiced in the bathhouses of the 1970s in America. It simply was first diagnosed in American gay men because of the advanced health care system in the United States and the economic status and social prestige of many of those whose cases appeared in 1981. It was not a "gay disease," as Jerry Falwell once claimed, although he was unfortunately correct in seeing it as a modern plague.

In the United States, however, AIDS is still a grave danger to the gay community. Figures reported by the Centers for Disease Control in August 1999 showed an estimated 28,000 cases of HIV infection among men and 12,000 among women per year. And while the rate of infection for gay men has dropped to around 6 percent annually in several major cities, including Baltimore, Denver, Houston, Los Angeles, Miami and New Orleans, the number of infections among gay men showed a slight rise in 1998 after dropping dramatically during the 1990s, largely due to the effects of practicing safe sex. What's more, the rise among younger gay men, ages fifteen to twenty-two, was found to be "alarming" in several major cities. Half of the new cases, or 3 percent, were found among this group alone.

In New York City, AIDS deaths had dropped 25 percent in 1998, according to the New York City Department of Health, after having already gone down a total of 65 percent in 1996 and 1997 combined. Yet they did not decline at all during the second half of 1998 or the first half of 1999. Many health officials in New York and elsewhere, expected the rate of infection and the number of deaths to start increasing again among gay men.

In 1998 and 1999, AIDS experts began warning of a new complacency among gay men about AIDS, brought on by the significant drop in the death rate over the previous few years and the apparent effectiveness of the new "drug cocktails" that had been developed during the 1990s. Editorials in major newspapers quickly picked up on this theme, and warned against a return to risky sexual behavior. Such warnings were not entirely appreciated. Greg, who is thirty-seven and lives in Houston, said to me, "The nannies are at it again." Greg has been practicing safe sex since 1984, and remains HIV negative, but he admitted that he isn't as careful as he used to be. "I am tired of being condom poor," he said. "It depends on who my partner is, but sometimes I don't use them now. I use my judgement." When I suggested, rudely, that roulette also involved judgement calls, he hung up on me. A month later he called me back. "Okay," he said, "You're right. A guy I was sure was okay, and wouldn't have played it safe with if I could have landed him in bed, turns out to be HIV positive. And he wasn't admitting it, either. A guy I know found out by accident when they were both in the same waiting room at a doctor's who specializes in AIDS."

There are a lot of Gregs. In San Francisco, there are gays pressing to change the rule and get the city to allow unmonitored sex in the sex clubs that have replaced the baths. In 1997, the city adopted a policy unique in the country. Sex is allowed in the approximately dozen clubs in operation, provided it is performed in public. Monitors must be able to check to see that sex partners are using condoms, which are available at the club. Safe sex information and rules must be posted. Some of the clubs actually have glass walls to facilitate the "oversight" duties of the monitors.

The "performance" aspect of these clubs, in several senses of the word, attracts gay men who like being watched while having sex, but keeps others away. Roger is a San Francisco resident who likes the clubs just fine. "I love being watched," he says. "And that's not just because I have a big dick. I know guys who have only five-and-a-half inches but like being watched, and guys with nine who don't. It's a mind thing, not just your physical attributes. So I understand why some guys would like to have the baths reopened and be able to have sex in private cubicles."

A 1999 movement to reopen the baths in San Francisco sparked a heated debate. Proponents of this change in the law focus on the fact that many gay men do not like to be watched and thus engage in unsafe sex in cars or public toilets. Bathhouses with private cubicles, they maintain, and with safe sex information and condoms readily available, would give such men a place to go have sex in private while at the same time promoting safer sex. Public officials and many gays are dubious about this rationale, and in a city that suffered so deeply from AIDS, they believe that reopening the bathhouses would increase the false sense of security that is creeping into the gay community.

Roger sees it that way too. "There are an amazing number of guys here who act like AIDS isn't a threat anymore. Some of them think the new drug combinations are working so well that you can become affected and still live until you're seventy. And of course there's the drop in new cases. Less than ten years ago, there were twenty-five hundred new cases and now there are only six hundred. Wow, only six hundred! It's especially bad among the really young guys, in their late teens or early twenties. They're as horny as hell, I know, I've been there, but they don't know what it is like to have thirty friends die in the space of two years. I try to tell them but they don't want to hear it."

Public health officials keep emphasizing that the new drug cocktails don't work for everyone, that no one knows yet how long they will be effective even for those who are being greatly helped now, and that an AIDS vaccine is still years away. But they are also keenly aware that young men just getting into the gay sex scene, especially in the big cities, are all too often in denial about the risks of unsafe sex and the horrors of full blown AIDS that does not respond to drugs. And even as they urge increased efforts at AIDS education, health officials know that complacency is difficult to fight. Roger puts it succinctly: "The best AIDS education there ever was came with the phone call saying another friend was dead."

Thus the next few years may well prove crucial in terms of the control of AIDS in the United States. There is no question in the mind of any expert that in Africa and the Far East the twenty-first century is going to bring untold millions of deaths from the disease. It is too widespread for there to be any other outcome. The drug combinations that proved so effective in the United States in the last four years cost as much as $15,000 per year for a single person. That, it has been pointed out, is equivalent to the total income of whole villages in Central Africa. An AIDS vaccine may come in a few years, and many avenues of research are being explored. A handful of men have been found whose immune systems seem to be able to kill the AIDS virus, and they are being studied intensely. But year after year, international AIDS conferences conclude that optimism about an AIDS vaccine is misplaced, as promising initial results repeatedly end in failure. Even if an AIDS vaccine were found tomorrow, it would take many years—even decades—to wipe it out around in the world in the way smallpox was finally eradicated.

In the United States, the steady decline in deaths and new HIV infections has been a reason to rejoice in the gay community, and extremely heartening to the medical community. But the clear signs that complacency is setting in, combined with evidence that very young men are not taking the risks of AIDS seriously enough, raises questions about where we are headed. For American gays, will AIDS be primarily a twentieth century plague, or will it become a twenty first century one as well? There are stirrings once again in the gay community of the bitter debate of the 1980s as to whether gay rights are a matter of social liberation or sexual license. They have surfaced in the arguments about reopening the San Francisco bathhouses. They are implied in the fact that in the bathhouses of New York, where supposedly only mutual masturbation is allowed, oral and anal sex is reported to be taking place quite commonly, according to the gossip among gay men. Several New York City gays told me such stories, often remarking, "There are a lot of young guys who don't care about the rest of the gay rights agenda. It's all about sex for them. Gay marriages, gay adoption, gays being allowed to serve openly in the armed services—they couldn't care less."

Such gays may be courting more trouble than contracting AIDS, some gays who lived through the 1980s believe. On December 9, 1999, the centers for Disease Control announced new guidelines that instructed states to report HIV Cases with the names of patients or identifying codes attached. According to the agency, nearly 900,000 Americans are currently affected with the virus, 297,000 of those having full-blown AIDS, making it important to track the spread of the disease more accurately. Although such information will be kept in a database requiring two passwords in order to protect the privacy of patients, such a step is regarded as alarming by some gay AIDS groups. One of the central political battles of the AIDS crisis during the 1980s was the fight to prevent such a database from being created. A central repository of patient names was regarded as both threatening and ill-advised in terms of trying to control the spread of the disease.

The threat involved stemmed from the fact that some politicians and leaders on the religious right who were calling for such a directory were considered perfectly capable of advocating "health camps" for gay men with the virus along the lines of the internment camps for Japanese-Americans during World War II. But gay leaders were also deeply worried that a great many gay men would not get tested for AIDS because they would be afraid of what might happen to them if their names were known to the federal government. There were plenty of gays who said they'd rather die than end up in a concentration camp, while far more feared that their names would be leaked, and that they would lose their jobs or be forced out of a closeted existence as a result. This was one of the few issues that all the major gay organizations could agree on at the time, and their united front persuaded government officials at all levels that the spread of AIDS would become less rather than more controllable if such a central directory was established.

The December 1999 guidelines from the Centers of Disease

Control have raised such concerns anew. If the incidence of HIV infection starts rising significantly, it might not be possible to control the uses to which a central directory could be put this time around. Brock, a computer expert who is gay, put it this way, "We didn't have the Internet back in the 1980s, or all these hackers who are so good at breaking into government computer files. It scares me to think what could happen if AIDS became a larger problem than it is." Brock's lover is a civil rights lawyer, and he raises another question. "If the country gets fixated on AIDS again, all other issues go out the window for years. You can forget about progress on gay adoption and gay marriage. We'll be fighting that same one-issue battle we were in the 1980s about gay sex habits. And you'd end up with the same divisions in the gay community. Trust me, we'd need to have Larry Kramer, or somebody like him, screaming at the top of his lungs that gay rights isn't just about sex, sex, sex. And you'd have other guys denouncing Larry or whoever it turned out to be this time as a traitor. I don't want to go through that again. The divisions are still there, they're just papered over because AIDS has been on the wane. Please let the next couple of decades be about progress on gay civil rights and not about AIDS and the alleged promiscuity of every gay man on the planet. There are an awful lot of guys out there who want to get married to each other, and that goes for our lesbian sisters, too. There are guys who want to adopt kids, and that's a crucial issue for lesbians who already have kids. Please let the next century be about them. Pretty please."

No one in the gay community would disagree with this fervent hope that AIDS become less and less of a problem, but not everyone shares the sense that gay liberation really isn't about sex. "You know," says Sparky, a forty-one-year-old commercial artist, "that battle really hasn't been won yet. The straight world still has this belief that gay men are extremely promiscuous, but they look the other way when straight men are. Look what happened when Magic Johnson revealed that he had AIDS. He got it because he'd had sex with something like 10,000 different women, and obviously some of them could have been HIV-positive because of sex with men who were, or through shared needles. I'll buy that. But there wasn't any outcry about his promiscuity. The straight guys at work were envious, not putting him down for having all those women. But if a gay man has 200 different partners in a year, he's some irresponsible sex maniac.' I say wait a minute, there something wrong here. Some gays are very promiscuous, sure, but so are an awful lot of straight men. A gay man has lots of sex with strangers, hey that's disgusting, but a straight man, wow, congratulations on being such a stud. Sorry, but that attitude's got to change."

I asked dozens of gay men and lesbians if they thought gay men were more promiscuous than straight men, and the vast majority, including the lesbians said no. Yet there is no question that the general public would answer that question with a yes. Sparky gets angry about that. "There's a double standard about this subject, and somebody like Larry Kramer—who seems to me to just hate the fact that he's gay, down deep—reinforces that idea. We still need to force the straight world to take a good look at itself and say, 'Well gays aren't any different in their sexual appetites from us, in the end. Some people, gays and straights alike, don't like sex at all; they think it's dirty or they just don't have much of a sex drive. Fine, but maybe that's their problem. Most human beings—gay or straight—seem to want regular sex but aren't hyper about it. And some people have to have a great deal of sex or they get real unhappy. Because the AIDS epidemic started off with gays who had a great deal of sex, the idea that we're all sex-crazed got even more implanted in the public mind. That needs to be changed. It's very important, unfinished business, and I wish there were more gay leaders and writers talking about it, nonstop. I don't give a damn about gay marriage, but I am not against it. The thing is that one of the reasons the general public thinks it's nuts is that they're still convinced that gays are sex maniacs. Get that cleared up first, and gay civil rights on other issues would be a lot easier to win some points on. AIDS stopped gays cold on making the case on sexual needs, and it's time to get back on the subject. That should be the first thing we deal with in the twenty first century."

three

Coming Out

When my book *Straight Women/Gay Men: A Special Relationship* was published by Dial Press in 1980, I headed up to Boston for a very long day of radio and television interviews. I began the day with a 7:40 a.m. appearance on a morning television show, did a full hour as the only guest on a noon TV program that mixed news snippets with my interview, recorded a radio and television session during the afternoon for subsequent broadcast, and ended the day—or began the next one—with an hour and a half appearance on Boston's hippest late night TV program, which began at one in the morning. The following morning I did two more radio shows. The hour-long show the first day and the two radio programs on the second day were call-in shows, and on all of them either a host or a caller asked if I was gay. I said, "Yes, I am." On the other programs there was a clear assumption on the part of the hosts that I was gay.

Returning to New York, where I had lived for fifteen years, I went down to the Village and stopped in the Oscar Wilde Bookshop, introduced myself to owner Craig Rodwell, and asked if he would like me to sign copies of my book. He glared at me and said, "Oh, yes, you. Are you gay or not?" Slightly taken aback, I replied, "Yes, of course I'm gay." "Then why doesn't your bio on the back say so?" he asked, sounding even more belligerent.

"Because my publisher didn't want the bio to say that," I explained. I began to understand what the problem was. "Look," I said, "I've been out for years. You can't possibly read the book and think otherwise. I've just been up in Boston telling people on both radio and television that I'm gay. One of the programs, I was told, reached a million Massachusetts viewers every weekday noon. That's hardly being in the closet, for God's sake."

"Well," he said, "Okay then. But next time be sure the jacket says you're gay." He then went off into the storeroom and brought out a dozen copies of my book to sign.

It is now 1999, and when I first picked up a copy of the massive history of the Gay Rights Movement in America, *Out for Good,* published this year, I noticed with some amusement that the jacket bios of the authors, Dudley Clendinen and Adam Nagourney, gave no indication of whether they were gay or not. Given the subject matter, I assume they are, just as I expected people to assume I was back in 1980. But, to tell the truth, it is a little annoying that they don't make the matter clear. I understand where Craig Rodwell of the Oscar Wilde Bookshop was coming from twenty years ago.

In 1980, of course, coming out was still a much bigger deal than it is now. Maybe we've reached the point where it's so completely understood that anyone who writes a book on gay history or gay issues is gay that there's no need to say anything. But I doubt it. Things have changed, but there are still a great many gays and lesbians who, while not exactly in the closet, aren't fully out either. And there are still plenty of people who are very much in the closet. Who's out and who's not, and why, is a subject that tells us a lot about how far we've come and how far we have to go.

Let's begin with famous people. When I began working on this book I asked dozens of gays and lesbians a question: If you hear that a celebrity is gay, do you immediately pass on the rumor or do you try to check it out first? Only a couple of people replied that they did any further checking, and frankly I don't believe them. Passing on a rumor that someone famous is gay is an almost irresistible impulse within the gay community, for reasons that can be both frivolous and deeply serious, sometimes both at once.

I was born in 1938 and came of age in the 1950s, a time which (pay attention, younger readers) was every bit as awful, particularly for gays, as it is so often painted. The fact that so many conservative politicians seem to have a nostalgia for the period can seem a kind of madness to gays who lived through it. The word "gay" itself had no public currency at all. There are debates about when and how it came into currency within the homosexual community, but even as late as 1969 the *Village Voice,* of all places, refused to print it on the grounds that it was obscene. Like multitudes of other very young gay men who were trying to find out if there was anyone else like them, I discovered that the definition of homosexuality in the 1950s, in any dictionary or encyclopedia I could find, included such words as "pervert" and "deviant." I was sufficiently self-confident to realize that while I might be different, I wasn't all *that* bad. At twelve, I experimented with a couple of other boys my age, and they'd seemed to have fun, too, so I wasn't completely alone. But I also quickly realized that what I wanted to do with other boys was not what most of them had in mind for the afternoon, and I'd better keep quiet about my desires. And so the search began for evidence that there were grown-ups (men, of course—it would be a while before I cottoned onto the idea that there were girls who wanted other girls) who were like me.

I was a voracious reader, way ahead of most kids my age, and I discovered Oscar Wilde and Andre Gide in my mid-teens. Oscar Wilde had gone to jail, but that was at the end at the previous century, and in this one Andre Gide had actually won the Nobel Prize. That was extremely reassuring, especially since I knew I already wanted to be a writer. But there was a question in my mind: was homosexuality peculiar to writers, or were there actors and politicians and sports stars who were like me too? There were hints, rumors, overheard comments from adults, but if there were a lot of famous homosexuals out there, they were certainly keeping awfully quiet about it. There were people I hoped were "queer" but was sure were not. In 1956, at age of seventeen, I went to see *Bus Stop* with my girlfriend. (I liked parties and I liked to dance, and I liked girls, as people, and Kathy never seemed interested in anything more than a goodnight kiss, although she got married during her second year at college.) There was a scene in *Bus Stop* where Don Murray was lying on the floor of his hotel room, talking about Marilyn Monroe's Cherie with his manager, played by Arthur O'Connell. Murray was doing sit-ups during the scene, wearing only long johns. There was a large bulge at his crotch, and every time he sat up, it kind of bounced and seemed to get bigger. There was one camera shot almost straight up between his legs that caused women in the movie theatre to squeal, even yelp. Kathy said, "What are they yelping about?" I said I didn't know, but in that moment any remaining doubt about my sexuality was forever cleared up. I wanted to tear those long-johns off Don Murray and get at that bouncing flesh underneath. That shot, by the way, has totally disappeared from the movie. The whole scene is chopped up on television to protect the home viewer from Murray's basket but you won't find the crucial shot in video versions, either.

So okay, I told myself, Murray almost certainly isn't queer, but some of those other guys must be. But which ones? As the years went by, the rumors would fly. Tab Hunter, they'd say. Fine but not really my type. Cary Grant, in spite of all those wives. That's interesting, but it was impossible to imagine having sex with Cary Grant. Alain Delon swung both ways, it was said. That was much more like it—in fact that was it—*Purple Noon, Rocco and His Brothers,* that shower scene, sigh. James Dean. Yes indeed. Marlon Brando, the rumor mill said. Sure, when he was younger. But then the truth would come out about someone and it would be the last person you suspected.

Randolph Scott! When I was a kid, I sometimes went to Saturday afternoon matinees of westerns with friends. But if there was a

Randolph Scott picture, my mother always wanted to go too. She had a thing about Randolph Scott; my father had one about Rhonda Flemming; they joked about it. By the time I found out about Randolph Scott I was in my thirties, and it only confirmed something I had long since learned from experience: you couldn't always tell a gay man by his mannerisms. If you're in the same room with someone, you can sense it, but up on the screen, well, that's more difficult— luckily for many stars.

Rock Hudson? America was stunned. Many gays were surprised too, even though there had been rumors. I heard it from an old friend in Los Angeles, who heard it from a friend who had been at a party where a guy he knew was matched up with Rock. "If you're interested, just go upstairs, he'll be waiting for you in the second bedroom on the left." Such stories were later confirmed, but when I first heard it, I thought well, maybe, although the question marks didn't keep me from passing the story on. So much of the "truth" about people being gay or lesbian was like that—you heard it from a friend of a friend of a friend.

On the other hand, I also told my own stories. When I was eighteen, Emlyn Williams, author of *The Corn is Green* and noted actor, came to Phillips Academy, Andover, to perform his celebrated one-man show about Charles Dickens. My father taught American History at Andover, and also headed the lectures and entertainment program. After the performance, as was the case with all performers in what was called "The Celebrities Series," Williams came to our house for a small party. He came with his wife, but he spent a long time talking to me. I knew he wanted me sexually—in the same room, as noted before, you can tell—and it embarrassed me. Partially that was because I had never felt such waves of lust directed at me in the presence of my parents, but the presence of his wife also made me uncomfortable. Since his death, Williams's homosexuality has been discussed in many books on the theater and the movies, but I knew back in 1957 because I could *feel* it.

Rumor, gossip, and, occasionally, certain knowledge because you or somebody you really trusted had been approached by or had sex with a celebrity. But the full story usually didn't come out until the celebrity was dead. Writers, as always, tended to be franker sooner—Tennessee

Williams, Truman Capote, Christopher Isherwood, James Baldwin. But movie stars and sports icons? No way.

A great deal has thus been made of the coming out of Sir Ian McKellen, Rupert Everett, Ellen DeGeneres and Anne Heche in the last few years. McKellen, an important and greatly gifted actor, but not really a star, is by far the frankest of these four much-ballyhooed figures. But even he admits that he waited until he was knighted to take the plunge. He has also said coming out has been a plus for him, not only personally because it made his life much simpler, but also professionally. Coming out got him American television exposure he might not otherwise have had, as he became a sought-after talk-show guest, and that fed into greater box office clout. Everett, for all his smoldering good looks, is also more of a character actor than a star, and the movie-going public has seemed quite blasé about the revelation that he is gay.

DeGeneres is the only one who managed to create something of a "scandal" by coming out, and that clearly has to do with the fact that she was starring in a television sitcom at the time. Because her show could be seen in "every living room in America," as the old cliché goes, the right wing decided to get quite exercised about what this might do to their precious children. Unfortunately for DeGeneres, her show was far from being viewed in every living room in the country either before or after she came out. And because the character she played on the show came out simultaneously, more sophisticated cultural analysts, and the gay community in general, tended to see the whole fracas in the press as something of a publicity stunt. Still, coming out as a commercial tie-in was something new, and suggested to many commentators that progress had indeed been made in terms of public acceptance of homosexuality, despite the caterwauling on the right wing. The ratings of her show, *Ellen,* actually increased for a while, but then sank fast. Some attributed the show's subsequent low ratings simply to bad scripts, although some critics thought that the problem lay in the fact that it had come to focus too exclusively on the character's sexuality. That left unanswered a major question: could a truly well-written sitcom with a gay or lesbian central character become a major hit, like

Seinfeld or *Fraiser.* There have been few indications that it could, although *Will and Grace* on NBC, with a gay male lead character of the "could-pass-for-straight" variety and a "screaming queen" second banana, managed to get renewed for a second season and indicated that the networks were willing to take some chances.

In some ways, the most interesting of these four cases was Anne Heche, Ellen DeGeneres's "love interest," as the media likes to put it. A fine actress with a broad range who had managed to steal several movies in secondary roles, she was on the verge of co-starring in the romantic comedy adventure *Six Days, Seven Nights* opposite Harrison Ford when the news that she was involved with DeGeneres broke. Ford was immensely supportive, in a low-key way that emphasized a "so-what" take on the issue. The movie got good reviews, Heche excellent ones, and it scored solidly if not spectacularly at the box office. But Heche is not necessarily a good measure of the public's willingness to accept a lesbian leading lady in a straight romantic role. As David Ehrenstein points out in his juicy, highly entertaining but fundamentally serious 1998 book *Open Secret (Gay Hollywood 1928-1998),* Heche was known to have been previously involved in heterosexual affairs, and there was a sense in Hollywood—and perhaps among the public as well—that she was "bisexual." In other words, the right man might be able to take her away from DeGeneres, an idea that fits nicely with a lot of heterosexual male fantasies. A little mystery never hurt any movie star, provided the mystery is open to personal interpretation on the part of the movie-goer.

Moreover, while the fact that *any* movie actor or actress should be advertising their homosexuality is a step in the right direction, no major star has yet declared himself or herself. To judge from the rumor mills, there ought to be a long line of big names forming to the left, but so far that line exists subliminally. In *Open Secret,* David Ehrenstein spends an entire chapter on Tom Cruise and Richard Gere without really getting anywhere. And they might even be the wrong suspects. Remember Rock Hudson. A Hollywood writer I talked to said, "There's always this problem of the difference between who gays would like to believe is gay, because they have fantasies about them, and who is really gay. Think about Charles Laughton—nobody was hot to trot with him. My personal choice would be Christian Slater or Kevin Bacon, but no such luck in any shape or form. But someday there'll be as big a shock as Rock Hudson, except that it'll be somebody at the height of his career. Then we'll see how the public really feels. These days it's hard even to get hold of reasonable rumors. The stars are much more careful than they were back in the days when Cary Grant and Randolph Scott were sharing house. I'm out in terms of my colleagues, but I'm too old and not famous enough for the press to care about, and anyway I've had the same partner for 16 years. Still, I am going to ask you not to use my name because I don't want to pestered for a lot for quotes."

Quite a number of people were willing to talk to David Ehrenstein on the record, but they were people who were already out very publicly in most cases, and in almost all cases were behind-the-scenes people: agents, production specialists, and the like. Many of them take note of the fact that it is easier to be out when you're not famous. The problem is, of course, that in our celebrity-crazed society, if you're not famous you don't count. So the assistant producer of a blockbuster action movie is gay? The public yawns. That changes no perceptions. It's when a famous person comes out, someone the public feels connected with, that attitudes began to shift, as they so clearly did when Rock Hudson was revealed to have AIDS.

Sir Ian McKellen delivers himself of a quite malicious riff in *Open Secret* on the subject of people whom everyone "knows" to be gay but who have never managed to quite say the words. He is particularly tart on the subject of Lily Tomlin. "I think Lily Tomlin would say that she's out, but she's not out. And goes to great considerable lengths to avoid being out." He then relates a story about how she was supposed to declare herself when she did a narration for *The Celluloid Closet.* Armistead Maupin, the scriptwriter for the 1995 documentary and the author of *Tales of the City,* wrote the speech for her, but she cut it. Tomlin has of course been a major fundraiser for AIDS causes, and it was her participation and ability to raise money that got *The Celluloid Closet* on track, but there are many people in the business, and in the gay community in general, who find it extremely irritating that she won't fully, openly declare herself.

But this is an area where hypocrisy can rear its head. I have talked to a number of gays and lesbians who have said that it annoys them that someone like Lily Tomlin or Rosie O'Donnell (who is widely assumed to be a lesbian even by many of her devoted middle-class heterosexual fans) just won't *say* it. Yet these same people are not really out themselves. They say they can't be because of their jobs. "I'm a teacher, I'm a minister, I am a pediatric nurse. . . ." It is difficult not to sympathize with such individuals. Their professions do present real problems in terms of coming out. An openly gay teacher below the college level, particularly in the public schools, is asking for trouble by coming out. I was once on the talk show *Sylvia,* when it was based in Detroit and before it appeared on CNN. I got an extra twenty minutes talking about my book *Straight Women/Gay Men* because the plane bringing in boxer Sugar Ray Leonard was delayed. I took questions from the studio audience, and one was about how people were likely to react when someone came out. I said that in urban areas, many people who came out were surprised by how little fuss it caused with friends and even employers, because in many cases other people had surmised the truth the truth for themselves. Sylvia interjected, "Except for teachers. Don't come out if you're a teacher." I immediately concurred. There are many gays in sensitive professions who must be as wary today as they were twenty years ago. But while their caution is certainly understandable, it makes the irritation they express about someone like Lily Tomlin somewhat unpalatable.

To put this double-standard in perspective, let's consider the in-the-closet existence of another kind of celebrity, the sports star. Way back in 1977, a former pro-football player named Kopay published an autobiography, *The David Kopay Story,* written with Perry Deane Young, in which he talked frankly about his own homosexuality and suggested he was far from being the only NFL player who was gay. His book caused a sensation at the time. Gay football players? Was this even possible? That was, of course, a straight world reaction. Most gay men had encountered more than a few homosexual football or baseball players along the way, even though they had been high school or college stars and not professionals. But at the time, the general public was thoroughly under the sway of the myth that gays were always effeminate, and that a macho professional athlete was bound to be straight.

In the intervening years, a number famous athletes have come out, but not those involved in macho all-American sports like football or baseball. The public had enough trouble dealing with the revelation of tennis great Billy Jean King's lesbianism, but she paved the way for an easier acceptance of Martina Navratilova. The homosexuality of Olympic diving legend Greg Louganis had been rumored for a long time, even in the mainstream press, before he came out in 1996 and told the world he was HIV-positive. By this time, the public was mature enough about the subject to generally respond to Louganis's revelation with sympathy, with studio audiences responding to him warmly on talk shows and his autobiography becoming a national best-seller. But in the almost quarter century since David Kopay's autobiography only a couple of second-rank NFL or Major League Baseball players have come out—after their playing days were over. Billy Bean, the former Detroit Tiger, Los Angeles Dodger, and San Diego Padre who came out in 1999, said that he had been "perfectly comfortable in the closet" as a player, but the great lengths he went to in keeping his homosexuality secret suggest considerable fear. Such fears may well be justified. Quite aside from locker-room nervousness among fellow players, there are a lot of beer-swilling rowdies among baseball fans who might be expected to unmercifully jeer any openly gay player on the field. The fan base for tennis players and Olympic swimmers is of a very different sort, generally better-educated and better behaved.

At the opposite end of the spectrum from football and baseball, there is figure-skating. There is a general assumption on the part of the public, apparent in the attitude of sportscasters who have to grit their teeth and report the results of the National, World, and Olympic competitions, that most male figure-skaters are gay. This is not in fact the case. Because of my sister's involvement in the sport, I got to know many of the great skaters of the 1950s and 1960s, and wrote an encyclopedia of the sport that was published in 1997. Homosexuality among male figure skaters is slightly more common than in most sports, but many of the greatest skaters are straight. The grace that is inherent in figure-skating is, however, too easily confused with effeminacy by the ignorant, and for the benighted it can obscure the enormous athletic prowess necessary to perform triple and quadruple jumps—although it should quickly be added that a gay male skater can be just as athletic as a straight one. Skating became an enormously popular sport on television, and it's obvious that most viewers don't care whether a skater is gay or not. Again, the fan base tends to be better educated and better mannered. But even so, gay skaters are very closeted, and often go to considerable lengths to obscure their homosexuality. Football and baseball players may fear the reaction of rowdy fans, but why should skaters even worry about it?

A famous and very popular former medal winner who is now a professional agreed to talk to me strictly off the record. "The whole gay business is a big problem in figure skating," he said. "There are straight male skaters who go a little bonkers because they know their public assumes they are gay, and they go on and on about the women they're dating or the kid they have because they are so paranoid on the subject. There are others who just ignore it. For those of us who are gay, it's a big subject for discussion. Rudy [Gallindo] was a special case—he lost both his brother and coach to AIDS and was out when he wasn't winning. I'd like to be out, but there's terrific pressure against it in the skating world. There's an awful lot of money involved in the sport these days, because of television, and our agents, skating officials, and sometimes our families are afraid we'll kill the goose that lays the golden egg. At the top level, there are certainly more straight skaters than there are gay ones, but a lot of people in the sport think there are just enough of us so that if we all come out, skating would forever be labeled a 'gay sport.' And nobody wants that. It's completely unfair to the many straight guys in the sports. You'll notice that almost all the big money endorsement contracts go to the ladies, though. Advertisers are terrified they'll make a mistake and pick a guy who's gay and will be outed down the line. And what would that do to soup sales? And if we got labeled as a gay sport, would even the ladies get those endorsements?

We're closeted, those of us who are gay, yes, but we often feel as though we are locked in, and somebody on the other side has got the key."

Soup sales, indeed. It needs to be remembered that when Billie Jean King was outed, her endorsements went out the window. By the time Greg Louganis came out, advertisers made a big point of not yanking his endorsements immediately. But they were gone soon enough. You never saw Martina Navratilova pushing soups or colas or breakfast cereals. Those are products everyone buys, including several million right wingers, and no major brand wants a boycott on its hands because gay-bashing ministers or politicians say the morals of American kids are being undermined by the fact that a gay or lesbian sports star is promoting a breakfast cereal.

Money, all by itself, keeps a lot of celebrity gays in the closet, whether they are sports stars, movie stars, or television stars. Their celebrity is part of the problem. It's why they're rich, but it makes them bigger targets when anything in their lives goes wrong. All they have to do is shove a photographer and it can turn into national news in the utterly sensationalistic and trivialized journalistic world we now live in. The public may not know how to find Kosovo on a map, and even presidential candidates can get away with not knowing who foreign leaders are, because the average American doesn't know, either, and doesn't care. But everyone knows about it when a movie star gets caught with a prostitute. When Eddie Murphy was hauled in with a transvestite prostitute, he spent weeks trying to fight the notion that he might be gay, even though there was no evidence that anything sexual had occurred between them. Hugh Grant, caught in the middle of getting an actual blow-job from a female prostitute got off a lot easier. Even his girlfriend forgave him. It's the naughty heterosexual on the one hand and the deep secret revealed on the other. Grant could say he was just a horny guy making a mistake. Murphy was reduced to pleading that he was just giving a poor soul a ride, and no he wasn't, he wasn't—promise now—he wasn't *gay*.

But even with Hugh Grant, there was much speculation about whether he had become box office poison. It turned out he hadn't, and neither had Murphy. Both have had hits since their "scandals." But the fear remains for celebrities. The public is extremely fickle in its affections, always looking for a new hot fantasy date. You never know when they're going to turn on you, if you're famous, and the fear remains that coming out will give the public one of the best reasons to dump you for good.

So as always, we come back to what the public feels. And the news is not as reassuring as it might be. The polls make it very clear. The Gallup organization has been asking Americans for years about homosexuality. Back in 1977, only 13 percent of Americans thought homosexuality was something a person is born with. By 1998, that figure was up to 31 percent. Progress, yes, but 47 percent still believed that homosexuality was caused by upbringing or some other environmental factor—which implies that one could be turned back into a heterosexual. Even back in 1977, the public believed that homosexuals should have equal job opportunities, by a margin of 56 percent to 33 percent, and by 1996, 84 percent endorsed equal job opportunities. But—and it is a very big but—in 1998, 59 percent of Americans still thought that homosexuality is morally wrong.

It is very difficult to find a gay or lesbian who doesn't believe that the more people who come out, the more accepting the heterosexual majority will become of gays. In the decades since Stonewall that has become a core belief among gays and lesbians. It is nearly as widely believed that when a celebrity comes out, it does a particularly large amount of good. Gays point to the shift towards greater sympathy that grew out of Rock Hudson's exposure. But many gays I've talked with suggest that the coming out of celebrities varies in its impact according to who the celebrity is and how he or she is regarded by the public. Chris, a professor of sociology, makes this point with particular cogency. "If a baseball MVP or the quarterback of a winning Super Bowl team came out, it would have an enormous effect and do a great deal of good. If it's some Hollywood pretty boy, everyone would just shrug and say, 'Well, of course him. I always wondered.' It would have to be a really macho movie star to make such a difference. There's a great story about John Wayne I recall. When he was making *The High and the Mighty,* which his company was producing, he kept trying to tell the director, William Wellman, what to do. Wellman finally blew his stack and said, 'And you coming back here and doing my work is going to be just as foolish as my going up and doing your personality with that lousy fairy walk you've got.' That shut up Big John. He was straight as a pin, of course, but he did have a fairy walk. But if a John Wayne equivalent were gay and came out today, it would do a hell of a lot of good. But not some weirdo or pretty boy. You've got to throw the public for a loop by confounding their perceptions, not just confirm their suspicions."

There are also those who suspect that the period in which the revelation that a celebrity is gay could have great impact is just about over, except perhaps for a football or baseball star. From this point of view, the public is getting used to the fact that some famous person is going to come out or get outed every so often. The shock value is gone, and with it the opportunity to make people reconsider their prejudices. Laura, a high school English teacher, says, "Particularly with kids, even the ones who still call others faggots, the idea that somebody famous might be gay is big yawn. They all know about Elton John and K. D. Lang and Melissa Etheridge, after all. They either like their music or they don't. I suppose they could be thrown if it were somebody the girls were swooning over like Ricky Martin, or somebody who's too pure like Amy Grant. But if it were somebody like Ricky, the boys would say, 'I knew it, I knew it,' and with Amy Grant they'd roll their eyes and say, 'Everybody's a fake.' Don't get me wrong here, I haven't heard any rumors about either of those two, they're just examples of the kind of people whose outing might make a real impression."

Laura thinks the real difference will be made with people who are personally known—friends, neighbors—coming out. "Celebrities are so outsize to begin with that they're expected to be different, one way or another. But the plumber, or the local bank vice president, that would make people say, 'Gee, I hadn't realized how many ordinary Joes and Janes were gay. Maybe it's not all that strange, after all.'" Yet Laura has to admit with some embarrassment, that she is not fully out herself. "I shouldn't really be giving advice, should I? My family knows all about me, and my close friends, and I'm sure most of the people I work with. But I am not going to announce it from the stage of the school auditorium, or even write a letter to the local paper that says, 'I'm a lesbian and here's what I think.' I can't do that. There are parents in this town who'd be after my scalp, and I don't trust the educational bureaucrats who run things to protect me. They're cowards, every one of them, and they run for cover even if some idiot parent wants the Harry Potter books banned from the school library. But of course, I am a coward too. I don't want trouble, so I am still half in the closet. It's something I don't like about myself, but I am too afraid to take a leap."

▼ ▼ ▼

Almost everyone in the gay community may agree that coming out leads toward mainstream acceptability, but there are very divergent views about actually doing it. There has been a split on this issue from Stonewall on, with periods of intense infighting at regular intervals. A wave of activists came out in the early 1970s, taking charge of pushing the new gay agenda on the legal and political fronts. These individuals, some largely forgotten, some famous to this day, were all heroes in the sense that they were willing to put their reputations and their economic security on the line in support of gay rights. But, as in any movement, there were differences of opinion about how far to go at any given time. As we will see in the chapter on politics, moderates who specialized in working behind the scenes sometimes felt that their best efforts had been sabotaged by more radical activists who insisted on trying to get everything at once, and whose modes of protest could be flamboyant in ways that disgusted or infuriated the wider public. Men in drag in the visitor's balcony of a state legislature, as appeared in Minnesota, were not regarded as helpful by moderates trying to round up votes for a gay rights bill.

Flamboyance in general was something that many gays still in the closet found both worrying and personally upsetting. Now in his mid-fifties, George, a New York book editor, speaks for many on this subject. "I was still in the closet in the 1970s. I went to gay bars and the baths, but I kept very quiet about that at work and with my heterosexual friends, of whom I had quite a few. And I would just cringe when I saw the coverage on television of the Gay Pride March every year. I didn't march myself, but I went as a spectator a couple of times. If you were there, you'd see a lot of ordinary-looking men and women in the parade, but what they showed on television—both the local New York news shows and the national broadcasts—always focused on the drag queens and the boys wearing practically nothing and flaunting their baskets. I liked looking at those boys, some of them were gorgeous beyond belief. And I've always liked drag shows. But as part of a parade for gay rights they seemed to me to be sending exactly the wrong message. Especially since they knew damn well they'd be the ones who ended up on television."

George can laugh about it now, but he remembers how embarrassed he was when straight colleagues or friends brought up the parade in conversation. "I realize now that almost everyone knew perfectly well I was gay. But I thought I was passing a lot better than I was. Sometimes, people who brought up the gay pride parade were trying to rise out of me, I'm sure, but I think most of them were really curious about my reaction to the parade itself. I'd always say something about how television inevitably goes for the sensationalistic aspect of things, and they'd nod, but I am sure I was blushing. I would feel the blood in my face. And in a funny way, I used those prancing queens and nearly naked boys as an excuse not to come out. I'm not like that, I'd tell myself. I'm a respectable citizen. And off I'd go to the baths. Fortunately I was into oral sex, or I'd probably be dead by now."

There were a great many Georges in the 1970s and on into the early 1980s. Gay, yes, but oh so respectable—when they weren't at the bars or the baths. George remembers when the parade began to change, and his attitude as well. "It was in the mid-1980s when AIDS was raging out of control that you started seeing the parents marching with their sons, most of whom were HIV-positive, I'm sure. And I had a lot of friends who were dying, of course. It was time to come out, and join the parades out of respect for them. My straight friends, except for one couple who was terrified I'd infect their kids just by touching them—stupid people—were completely calm about it when I came out. My friend Iris, whom I had known since third grade, even sent me a card that read, 'Congratulations on your new status.' And she had kids too. That card made me cry, and I thought, 'why didn't I do this years ago?'"

Another man, one I've known for nearly thirty years, never could come out to his colleagues. I'll call him Brian. In the early 1980s, when he was already in his fifties, he was called to the offices of the CEO of the major New York bank where he worked in a senior capacity, heading an entire department. The CEO, a very important man whom I also happen to have met, is the kind of establishment bigwig who manages to be frightening even when he is trying to be charming. So I could well imagine the CEO's demeanor when he called Brian into his office that difficult day. Another unnamed senior banker, it seemed, had spotted Brian coming out of a famous gay bar in the company of a younger man. The younger man was in fact Brian's lover, and had been for a dozen years. They did not live together, however, because Brian was well aware that he had to be discreet.

He had not been discreet enough. Because he had been spotted coming out of a gay bar, and ratted on, the bank had hired a private detective to follow Brian. The CEO tapped a thick file on his desk and told Brian they knew a great deal about his private life. Because Brian did seem to be generally discreet, the bank would not fire him. He might well be given greater responsibilities in the future (Brian was very good indeed at his job), and commensurate salary increases, but he would never, ever be given a higher title than he had, and if there was the slightest hint of scandal, he would be discharged instantly. Brian caused no scandal—he was hardly the type—and he was indeed given greater responsibility and a larger salary in years to come. But even now, in his seventies, Brian can't look back on that day with equanimity.

George was afraid to come out for a long time; Brian was basically told by his employer to stay in the closet or else. The majority of gays in the 1970s and well into the 1980, were still in the closet even as the Gay Rights Movement was becoming a genuine political force and succeeding in getting at least some anti-discrimination legislation passed. Those in the closet often felt guilty. They were less likely to feel the self-loathing so prevalent in earlier decades, because it was evident that there were many gays who felt good about themselves and were unwilling to hide their sexual orientation. But fear of financial loss or social ostracism was still strong enough to deter a great many from declaring themselves to the world. And their guilt—not so much for being gay but for being secretive—was compounded by the fact that some gay activists, and most gay radicals, held those still in the closet in contempt.

Many gay men were forced out of the closet by AIDS. But even as the death toll mounted, there were those who went to their graves still undeclared. In the 1980s, the obituary pages were full of death notices that were misleading or ambiguous when it came to listing the cause of death. It was not always clear whether that was the result of orders left by the deceased or a matter of his family stepping in to protect their own names. Perusing the obituaries, many readers, whether out or closeted, would say to themselves or to a friend or lover, "Obviously it was AIDS." Sophisticated straights were perfectly capable of reading between the lines as well. Slowly things changed, as other men who were HIV-positive began to say to themselves that they did not want to have someone having to decode their own obituaries somewhere down the line. It became, strangely, more embarrassing to die in the closet than it was to come out while alive. At the end of the 1990s you could still come across the occasional coded obituary, but it was less and less usual, at least in the major cities. Yet it needs to be remembered that most deaths are not even recorded in major newspapers. So many "notable" gays, the kind of people who are accorded a write up in the *New York Times,* have died of AIDS in the past two decades—far too young in many cases—that obituaries we ought not to have read until sometime in the next century have long since appeared. With safe sex now being practiced by the majority of gays and the incidence of HIV infection down, with the effectiveness of the drug combinations keeping people alive much longer, gay men are no longer dying at a greatly accelerated rate. That leaves a question: how many coded obituaries will we be seeing ten years from now? Are we really seeing fewer of them at this point because so many gays are out? Will the older gays who escaped AIDS and who will die of strokes or cancer or heart attacks or other "natural causes" in 2012 be listing their long time companions as survivors?

There is no question that a great many more gays and lesbians are fully out today than before. They come from all walks of life, and all economic levels. Yet there are also legions of gays and lesbians who are only partially out—their friends and families may know, but not their employers. And even some friends and some family members may not be among the circle of those with whom it is felt wise to be completely open. I was surprised at how many of the dozens of gays I talked to while writing this book are not completely out. For many, the closet door is open, and if you pass by they might give you a little wave, or poke their heads out for a few words, might even step out and embrace the right passer-by. But they also stand ready to step back into the depths of the closet, shutting the door firmly as they do so, under certain circumstances.

Others seem to have a relationship with their gayness that is not unlike that of the married straight man or woman with an extra-marital affair. It's happening, but let's not discuss it, old friend, agreed? In cases like this, it's hard to know whether you're dealing with fear or shame or a sense of privacy—or a combination of all three. Is the caution or reticence just garden-variety human skittishness about being too frank about sex, or does it specifically relate to being gay, to having that kind of sex? The very fact that this question can be asked is clearly a sign of progress. Those of us who came of age in the 1950s remember when there was no question what was going on: you could see the panic in someone's eye as they thought they'd been found out, and there are few of us who lived through those times who did not occasionally experience such moments of panic ourselves. Now it is more often mere caution, and a degree of ambiguity, that you see in someone else's eye.

Even so, for the person who is fully out, such ambiguity in another person's eyes is usually cause for a flash of irritation. "Oh grow up," you want to say. Or, "Come off it, you don't need to play coy with me." Yet not many gays—only the radical few—seem truly angered by someone else's unwillingness to come out fully. In the 1980s, there was a period when some gay activists were intent on outing everyone in sight. "Stand up and be counted or else," was the cry from members of ACT-UP and other provocateurs. That stance did not go over well with the great majority of gays. It was felt to be inhumane, even cruel. Very few gays or lesbians I interviewed were in favor of forcibly outing other people, with the exception of public figures, politicians, or member of the clergy, for example, who were noisy gay-bashers yet suspected of being gay themselves.

Dean, who is in his late twenties and works in the music business, put it this way, "I live in Los Angeles now, and I am completely out. I'd be happy to declare myself on television if anybody cared. But when I was just out of college, I lived for three years in Milwaukee. I grew up in Wisconsin. My parents and brothers and sister knew I was gay, I came out to them when I was nineteen, but I didn't go around the small town we lived in declaring myself, and even in Milwaukee, I was out with some people and not with others. Here, for me, I don't need to worry about it in any way. But—and I think this is important—there's a guy I work with who's the way I was in Milwaukee. And there's a reason for it. He's Mexican-American, and he's got lots of family here in Los Angeles. He's out with his immediate family, but not with some of his relatives or some people he went to high school with. He knows they'd have a problem, and for their sake more than his, he doesn't want to flaunt his gayness with them. So I don't think any of us who are out have the right to say somebody else is a coward because they're only half out. Life is more complicated than that. You've got to give people some slack."

Among younger gays, an increasing number came out in their teens, like Dean. Some high schools in major cities have gay clubs, as do a number of private prep schools. When I was attending Andover in the 1950s, the very idea of a gay club would have been laughable. Not that

Andover had a gay bashing culture in general. There were teachers whom everybody assumed were gay, students and faculty members alike, but they were extremely circumspect. Most of those men would disappear to Europe in the summers, and who knew what went on there, but during the school year they were extremely careful. One who wasn't got fired, even though his indiscretion had nothing to do with a student and was never proved. He was able to get a job immediately at a lesser nearby school, where he stayed a couple of years before moving up the ladder again to teach at Choate, where he remained for the rest of his career. He became one of my closest friends in subsequent years, although never a sexual partner, since we simply weren't interested in each other.

There were boys at Andover who called others "faggots," but there weren't many who were name callers and they usually stopped after a while—it just wasn't acceptable at Andover to call people names. There was one kid who was openly gay. He was a good athlete, and very rich. I'll call him Stan. Stan once offered a scholarship boy in the dorm twenty-five dollars if he'd let Stan blow him. The whole dorm knew about the offer and told the scholarship boy to accept, because he could use the money. But the answer was no. Another boy announced he was able to blow himself. Nobody believed him, so he agreed to demonstrate. He—wouldn't you know—was straight. There was no question about it. Incidents like these, however, sometimes made me regret that I was a day student. I seemed to be missing out on a whole lot. In later years, I discovered that everybody was missing out on more than they knew. Two sets of roommates, athletes whom everybody thought were completely straight, were having torrid sex all through Andover and went right on doing it through college and after. One of these boys later married, causing heartbreak for his lover, but he had a reason. He stood to inherit several million dollars at age twenty-five, provided he was married. And so he went back into the closet for good.

The first person I came out to was a friend at Andover. He was extremely straight, and absolutely consumed by sex. He'd had his first sexual experience with a girl in a church choir loft in New York City when he was thirteen. He didn't tell many people about that, but he told me, and for reasons I can't explain even now, I knew I could tell I him I was a queer and he wouldn't bat an eyelash. I was right. "That's interesting," he said. "I'm glad you told me first. It's an honor."

"It's an honor." Maybe I was just lucky, although I have known other gays who've had similar experiences. Choosing who to come out to first remains, even now, all evidence suggests, a crucial decision. And for every boy or girl who comes out as a teenager to someone—friend, parent, teacher—and finds immediate calm acceptance, there is another for whom it will be traumatic. That fact is reflected in the gays and lesbians who get ostracized at school, or beaten up. It is reflected in teenage suicide statistics. For all the changes that have taken place, coming out at the wrong time, or in the wrong place, or to the wrong person can still be dangerous. The kids who have done it at fifteen or sixteen or seventeen in the past few years in cities and towns across the country know that. And for that reason, such boys and girls—especially those who come out fully, are heroes. Even for adults, coming fully out can be dangerous. It depends on the kinds of jobs they have, and where they live. Not everyone is up to being a hero. As Dean said, we need to give people a little slack. Yes, the more gays and lesbians who come out, the less dangerous it will be for others. That is certainly true. Yes, the gay plumber and the lesbian bank teller, when they are fully out, not only set an example for the gay community but make it easier for the heterosexual majority to understand that it is okay, and not really that strange, to be gay. Yes, it would help if more entertainment stars came out, and help even more if the gays in the NFL or Major League Baseball could be open. But circumstances can make things very difficult, and that needs to be recognized, too.

More kids are coming out every day, and more thirty-five-year-olds as well, and every one of them makes it easier for the next person to do the same. But it is a big country, and there are many places where bigotry remains deeply ingrained. It is to be hoped that the gay community has become mature enough as a whole to not only cheer those who do come out, but to respect the fears of those who hang back. If we have patience, the day will come, the twenty first century day, when it will no longer be necessary to feel such immense relief when a straight friend says, "I'm glad you told me first. It's an honor."

four

Gay Marriage

On May 1, 1991, two lesbian couples and a gay male couple filed suit in Hawaii asking for "injunctive and declaratory" relief because the state Department of Health had denied them marriage licenses on the grounds that the three couples seeking to marry one another were same-sex partners. Ninia Baehr, Genora Dancel, Tammy Rodrigues, Antoinette Pregil, Pat Lagon, and Joseph Melilio, the plaintiffs in the case, maintained through their lawyers that the refusal to grant them licenses was unconstitutional under the state's privacy guarantee and equal protection law, as set forth in the Hawaii Constitution. Thus began a nine-year legal saga that would bring same-sex marriage to the forefront as a gay civil rights issue, and would have legal repercussions in numerous states and at the congressional level.

Gay marriage was hardly a new idea. Way back in 1967, two years before Stonewall, gay marriage had been endorsed in a major speech by a woman named Rita Hauser. She said that laws prohibiting marriage between individuals of the same sex were unconstitutional. Noting that the rationale for such laws often turned on the belief that the chief purpose of marriage was reproduction, she declared that concept outmoded in an overpopulated world. With the rise of birth control as a social goal in many countries, new ways were constantly being sought to limit rather than encourage reproduction. "And I know no better way of accomplishing this than marriage between the same sexes," Hauser said.

Who was Rita Hauser? A gay activist? No. An artist with a bohemian outlook on the world? No. Mrs. Hauser was a prominent member of the New York political establishment, a noted Republican fundraiser and lawyer. She spoke in favor of same-sex marriage not at some gay organizational meeting, but at an American Bar Association forum in the subject of "Women's Liberation and the Constitution."

At the time, the liberal Republican Nelson Rockefeller was Governor of New York. But even he had bowed to an arm-twisting by the Roman Catholic Archdiocese of New York to retain the criminalization of homosexual acts and adultery when the state penal code was revised for the first time in ninety years. Thus, Rita Hauser's espousal of same-sex marriage was extremely forward-looking. It was not, however, quite so radical as it may appear to be now. I remember reading about her speech in the *New York Times,* and discussing it with a number of gay and lesbian friends. We were a bit surprised and a little amused—but took it as a welcome sign that things might be changing. There was some rumbling from the Archdiocese about Mrs. Hauser's statement, but not enough to keep her from being appointed as a delegate to the United Nations General Assembly by President Nixon in 1969. She has since had a wide-ranging career, serving on numerous prestigious committees involving international and human rights, teaching at Harvard's John F. Kennedy School of Government, and continuing an active role in Republican politics.

It is significant, however, that when Charles Kaiser, author of *The Gay Metropolis,* asked Mrs. Hauser in the mid-1990's to comment on her 1967 speech, she declined. That does not seem surprising. There are no more liberal Republicans, and even moderates often seem to be an endangered species. To bring up the subject of same-sex marriage in 1967 was somewhat daring; to reaffirm such ideas now would almost certainly cause a major ruckus on the Republican right. In 1967, Hauser was seen as making a feminist point rather than as a gay rights advocate. Betty Friedan's *The Feminist Mystique* had been published less than four years earlier, and the National Organization of Women had been founded only the year before. To advocate same-sex marriage was simply to let loose another arrow at the broad target presented by a male-oriented system of laws. Hauser's further point that same-sex marriage was a splendid way to help control the worldwide population explosion could be taken as a provocative way to get people to think more seriously about birth control issues. While Paul R. Erlich's apocalyptic book *The Population Bomb* would not be published until 1970, concerns about the subject were already widespread in 1967, and it was a subject about which Hauser was known to be concerned, one she would continue to emphasize as her distinguished career continued. Within the context of feminism and population control, Hauser' speech, while somewhat daring, was hardly the kind of clarion call for real social change that serves to give defenders of the status quo any serious nightmares. It could be said, and was in some circles, that the smart young married Republican lady was just showing off.

Those of us who has been somewhat surprised by the content of Rita Hauser's 1967 speech were considerably more astonished by the January 26, 1971, issue of *Look* magazine. A theatrical agent who was a friend of mine called me up and said, "Have you seen this week's *Look?*" I hadn't. "Better go get it," he said. "There's a married couple in it you'll be interested in." That's all Charles would tell me. Figuring the couple must be people I knew, I went down to the corner and bought the magazine, a theme issue on "The American Family." Flipping through it looking for a familiar face, I came across something unexpected: three pages devoted to two young men in Minnesota, profiled under the headline "The Homosexual Couple." That very month I had moved into an apartment in Long Island City, one stop on the F train across the East River from Manhattan, with Paul Baldwin, whom I'd met the previous May. We'd both had previous relationships that had lasted only a couple of years but this time. . . . We're still together nearly thirty years later, and although I had no certainty of that happy outcome in 1971, Charles had been right. I was very interested in the two men from Minnesota.

Their names were Jack Baker and Michael McConnell, and they were not in fact legally married, although there was a picture of them in *Look* applying for a marriage license. They'd been denied it, unsurprisingly, even though the Minnesota law said nothing about the sex of prospective marriage partners. The case was still in the courts. Baker and McConnell were shown not only being cuddly in the presence of straight friends, but also in conversation with their Roman Catholic priest—at church. The accompanying text went out of its way to inform readers that some homosexuals were involved in stable relationships instead of a life of "one-night stands in bathhouses, public toilets or gay bars. . . ."

This was quite something! Once again, though, some context is necessary. Both *Look* and its more successful arch-rival *Life* were beginning to lose readers at a rapid rate by 1970, as television became the main source of information for the American public. *Look,* in particular, was suffering, and trying to boost its sales by becoming more provocative than *Life.* The inclusion of Baker and McConnell in an issue on the American family was a clear example of editorial risk-taking. Other mass market magazines did not rush to follow suit with flattering portraits of gays, and although gay issues were receiving increasingly widespread coverage, simply because the protests and legal challenger mounted by activists had to be covered as news, the tone was often disparaging. The subject of gay marriage basically dropped from view, except in Minnesota, where the fallout from the Baker/McConnell case continued for some time. Once in a while a story would surface about a bishop closing a church or firing a minister because he was willing to perform a gay marriage. This happened in Washington, D.C., later in 1971, and in Boston in 1973, but gay marriage was seldom more than a side issue for years to come.

But the subject continued to rumble beneath the surface. Gays and lesbians would raise it in conversation, and occasionally an activist would raise it in a speech or manifesto. A few gays and lesbians actually did something about it. Here and there, couples exchanged rings and conducted some kind of service, but it was usually presided over by someone unconnected to any major church. During the 1970s and 1980s, there were a number of quasi-religious groups that ordained lay ministers, most of whom became involved as a way of avoiding taxes, a dodge that the IRS eventually clamped down on.

One couple who took this route are Stephen and Ross, who held a ceremony when they both were in their early thirties. They lived in California, where lay ministers abounded, and they were married in 1981 in Marin County, north of San Francisco, at a friend's small estate in a wooded area. Stephen recalls, "There was a long flagstone terrace where the ceremony was performed, with the guests gathered on a big sloping lawn below us. It was a perfect Saturday in September, and about fifty friends had driven up from San Francisco for the day. Ross's younger sister was there, but neither his parents or mine. We'd been living together for three years, and our parents certainly knew we were gay, but it was not something we discussed with them. That was more respectable back then—among gays I mean. A lot of people had that kind of relationship with their parents.

"Our 'minister' was a lawyer, a very smart guy who mostly represented underdogs, right across the spectrum. That meant he didn't make a helluva lot of money, and he'd gotten one of those mail-order ministries to shove it to the IRS. Anything that put a finger in the eye of the establishment he was for, and he was quite excited about marrying us. It was a first for him. We'd bought rings to exchange, simple gold bands, but we didn't wear them on the traditional finger. We'd made up our own service. We took the "have and to hold" part from the usual protestant service, because we liked it, but we were somewhat naughty about the rest of it. We did mention God, but not in the usual way. 'In the eyes of God,' we had Jack say, 'whoever he or she may be.' That got some applause from the women who were there.

"At the end of the service, Jack intoned, 'the grooms may kiss," and we did, to much cheering. We hadn't said the 'until death do us part' stuff because we thought it was hypocritical. But it wasn't just a lark or an excuse for a party. Ross and I were very serious about it, and even though we hadn't made the promise, we actually were faithful to each other. That well may have saved our lives because AIDS came along the next year—or at least it began to be recognized for what it was the next year. We'd already lost a friend to a weird succession of medical problems that in retrospect had to have been AIDS.

"Ross and I stayed together for eight years, which was as long or longer than most of our straight friends. By then we were in our early forties, which I think was a dangerous time emotionally for men in general, straight or gay. We both started to get a roving eye at the same time—although we were very careful about practicing safe sex—and so we were able to part as good friends. Still are, even though neither of us is all that taken with the other's partner. We meet for lunch mostly, and sometimes see one another at parties. When people ask if I was ever married, I always say yes. Sometimes I explain that it was to a man, sometimes not, depending on who's asking."

I asked Stephen if he and his current partner had considered getting married. "Not really. Now of course it's a big issue. Making same-sex marriage legal, having a real church wedding. I think that's great. But it's funny in a way. I had a friend once who dropped out of Princeton in 1960. He always added, 'Before it was popular.' I kind of feel that way about getting married. I did it. I did it sincerely, and I am glad I got married to Ross. It was pretty special back then. But of course I also got divorced. I wonder about that aspect of it. All these gays and lesbians who want the right to get married legally now, they don't talk about divorce much. A few of them do, the ones who are really into fighting it out in the courts. I don't think we'll get the legal right to marry without the legal entanglements of divorce. And I sometimes wonder whether people are going to like that complication much. Ross and I had an amicable split, as I say, but it was still a big problem dividing things up financially. It didn't get ugly for us, but it does for most people, I think. I wonder if people fully understand what they'd be getting into."

Stephen's final point is well taken. I have discussed the question of same-sex marriage with dozens of gays and lesbians over the past two years, and the range of responses has been very broad. Some people have thought the matter through with great thoroughness, but to very different conclusions about the importance of same-sex marriage. Others have strong feelings about the issue, both pro and con, that seem to be based more on a gut reaction than systematic analysis. Still others find themselves wavering, and sometimes changing their minds when the implications or the practical consequences of legalized same-sex marriage are delved into more deeply.

In exploring these various points of view, it seems appropriate to begin with the most dogmatic positions, pro and con. Once the extremes are established, it will be easier to discover where the middle actually lies and examine the potential for greater consensus. As is often the case with controversial issues, the most passionate responses are negative ones. Gay separatists often find the very idea of marriage anathema.

Spike has lived in the East Village of New York City for nineteen years, since dropping out of the University of Maryland after one term. He's an example of the kind of New York gay man who was more common in the 1960s and 1970s. He doesn't travel above 14th Street if he can possibly help it. Although he loves the theatre, he wouldn't be caught dead at a Broadway show, but helps to keep a number of experimental Off-Broadway shows alive, not just by buying tickets but also by helping construct stage sets for practically no money. An expert carpenter, he earns a living constructing built-in bookcases, custom cabinets, and room dividers for people renovating lofts and tenement apartments. His own rent-controlled apartment in a rundown building is a small masterpiece of the carpenter's art. Spike has never had a live-in lover, but there are two or three men he has sex with on a regular basis. That means when he is in the mood. "Sex is better if it's not too planned or too often with the same guy," he says. Strikingly handsome with brown hair and blue eyes, he has no problems finding willing partners for one-night stands. He does practice safe sex, but wishes it weren't necessary.

Spike has several lesbian friends, but very few straight ones. And if a straight friend has a child, Spike ends the relationship with great speed. "As soon as they become parents," he says, "they turn into somebody else, even the ones who don't pay all that much attention to their kids. I don't want to deal with that." He never spoke to his own father again after telling him he was gay, something his father, a plumber, found totally unacceptable. He did call his mother occasionally on the telephone, and since his father's death five years ago, he has gone back to Maryland to visit her about once a year, but she has never been to New York.

"My mother is a sweet lady," he says, "but my father was a beer-swilling jerk. Beer, sports, and thank you Ma'am sex once a week. It took him about a minute and a half of loud grunting to get it off. My poor mother might just as well have been a rubber doll." Spike thinks marriage is a totally corrupt institution, and that any gay or lesbian who wants to have anything to do with it is crazy. "You know," he says, "there was no marriage ceremony in the Catholic Church until the thirteenth century. Oh, sure, popes married a few kings and queens, but ordinary people just had a civil ceremony. The church got into the act because it was a way to control people even more. And men went for it because they were always looking for ways to keep their wives in line. It's all about power, always has been, always will be. I've known a few straight people who got along just fine for years living together without being married, and then they tied the knot and everything changed. All these power struggles sprang up overnight like dandelions. And if they had a kid, forget it. A marriage license is like a hunting license, an excuse to kill, emotionally if not physically."

If it's pointed out to Spike that marriage also carries with it some practical benefits in terms of insurance, Social Security, and the like, he just shakes his head. "Then let's fight to get those benefits without getting married. Hey, even Disney allows insurance for same-sex partners. More and more big corporations do. Let's make that universal. Let's work to get Social Security and pension benefits for the unmarried partners of people who've lived together a certain number of years. Leave marriage the fuck out of it."

Because Spike himself has never had a long-term partner, or even a short-term live-in partner, it is easy to suggest that he's simply a loner with antisocial tendencies, someone with a commitment problem, a man with psychological problems, even. Spike is far from unaware that he's vulnerable to such charges, however. "Look, I know I am not a good test-case. But there are plenty of straights who think marriage is for the birds, too, including a lot who've tried it three or four times. And I know gay partners who have the same view of marriage I do, people who've been together for a long time and obviously adore one another. I am not as peculiar as it may seem."

And in fact, Spike is correct in saying that there are long-term partners who are adamantly against the idea of marriage for same-sex partners. Dale and Harris have been together for twenty-four years, and have been resolutely faithful to one another. "We have had half a dozen three-ways," says Dale, "with friends we already knew well. We were all curious about one another and just decided to do it. It can be quite exciting to watch someone go down on your lover and then have Harris watch him go down on me. But we'd never have sex with someone else unless the other one was there taking part. We're the love of one another's lives, and we're lucky, I guess, to have found one another. But when people bring up the idea that we should get married, we just laugh. We try not to be rude about it, because sometimes the person who brings it up is very much in favor of same-sex marriage, but we think the whole idea is just silliness."

Harris elaborates. "We're sentimental about our relationship in some ways. Every year we celebrate the anniversary of the day we met, and next year, when we hit twenty-five years, we're going to have a big party—and we hope everyone brings lavish presents. But a big marriage ceremony? Never. That seems to us a subject for comedy, a parody of the straight world. Shouldn't one of us really wear a dress? And we don't have that kind of relationship, either sexually or psychologically. Nobody's in charge around here, nobody's the top all the time. We both have our special areas of strength, and we let the other take over when his talents are best suited to a social or business situation. But we're really equal, truly so, and I've met very few straight married couples I think that's true of. These days, sometimes it's the woman who is in charge, but usually it's still the man. Although in the case of older straight couples, sometimes the woman is actually the boss and just lets her husband think he is."

"My mother, for example," Dale puts in. "I remember when feminism was just getting going in the late 1960s, Anita Loos, who wrote *Gentlemen Prefer Blondes,* said it was crazy, women were throwing away an act they'd spend centuries perfecting, running the man but allowing him to think otherwise."

Harris admits that some of the gays and lesbians they know who like the idea of same-sex marriage appear to have quite equal relationships. But he echoes Spike by saying, "But wait until they do get married. One of them will start trying to take control, and there'll be problems. The thing is, marriage isn't really working well even for straights anymore. We have quite a lot of straight friends, and most of them have been married two, even three times. In one case, four times. When Dale and I had been together seventeen or eighteen years, things got a little difficult for a while, a lot of our friends were sort of quietly pissed off at us for being together so long. You know, you could see them thinking, 'What have those fags got that makes them so goddam solid in their relationships. It isn't *normal.*' Well it isn't normal for straights either. Two people who can love one another as much after twenty or thirty years as they ever did, maybe in somewhat different ways because they both grew as people, but just as completely, are unusual. We're very lucky, as I said before. But we certainly don't need to get married to prove it. At this stage, I think getting married would be a sign of insecurity. And there are straights who feel the same way. From what I gather, that's what famous couples like Susan Sarandon and Tim Robbins, or Jessica Lang and Sam Shepherd, feel about it, too. It's funny, really. Just as straights are beginning to recognize that marriage is just a way to keep weak people under control, for society and for individuals, suddenly a whole lot of gays and lesbians have decided it's a must. How silly you get?"

This kind of talks infuriates gays and lesbians who see the right to get married, whether legally or in the eyes of God, or both, as a central aspect of the human experience. Lois and her partner Mary have been together nine years, and are raising Mary's son from a youthful heterosexual marriage. "Marriage is as old as human history," says Lois. "As far back as we know anything at all, couples were getting married. The religion doesn't matter. The ancient Greeks and the Norse were getting married and they had gods who were married. Yes, yes. I know all about the exceptions, the polygamists and the rulers who engaged in serial marriage. But there's an innate instinct to pair off as couples and stay paired off. Even a lot of animals and birds do it, for heaven's sake. I'm a feminist to my toes, but one thing I don't buy is the idea that marriage is just something that got forced on is by patriarchal systems. Yes there have been too many cases where patriarchal systems took advantage of the instinct to form permanent pairs and twisted it into forms of excessive control over women, but that doesn't mean that the original instinct is false. It just got perverted sometimes as a way of making women knuckle under."

Mary, who has been nodding as Lois speaks, takes up the theme and extends it. "And homosexuals, women or men, have the same instinct for permanent pairing. Or at least a great many of them do. There are promiscuous men and women, and they can be straight or gay. Maybe they're sex addicts, maybe they're doing what their hormones demand. It doesn't matter. They're really the exception. Most human beings want to form a permanent pair with someone else, of the opposite sex or the same sex. It can be hard to find the right person sometimes. We think we have, but then it turns out we made a mistake. But we keep looking, most of us, hoping to find that partner, and when you do it's so right that it seems like a revelation. You may have been in love before, but now you realize that that was just a pale imitation of the real thing. And once you find the real thing, you not only want to keep it forever and ever, but you also want to sanctify it, because it deserves to be sanctified, by the church and by the law."

"The idea that only love between people of the opposite sex can be worthy of sanctification by the church, or be legally recognized is an insult to us as human beings," Lois says. "It's sheer prejudice."

"It's also insecurity," Mary adds. "A lot of married straights haven't really found the right partner, and they know it, and it's slowly killing them inside. And allowing a gay or lesbian couple to get married would make them feel even worse. It's like people who have had rotten sex all their lives, and can't stand the idea of other people having good sex, so they get all prim and proper and say sex is evil, or for having children period. My parents had to have had sex twice, because there's me and I have a brother, but they had separate bedrooms and there was almost no traffic between them when I was growing up. I know my mother found sex disgusting, and I think my father was just as glad, because he had a very low sex drive himself. They didn't speak to me for three years after I came out, but I don't think their shock was so much about my wanting another woman as my wanting sex, period. That I could arrange my life around sexual desire was just beyond them. And it made them angry, because I knew deep down they thought I was getting pleasure from something that didn't bring any to them. It's very strange, because they actually liked the idea of Lois and me getting married. I think they believe that if Lois and I got married we'd lose interest in sex."

Lois laughs at that. "Little do they know their daughter."

Mary smiles and says, "True enough. But it's also very important to us to get married as a celebration of everything we are together. It would be an affirmation of us, of Lois and Mary as union of body and soul. Marriage has been about that from time immemorial. And it shouldn't be denied to us just because we're of the same sex. It's not anti-family, the way the religious right says. It's pro-family. It's saying that families can be a great good in the world. I don't understand why they can't see that. For us to get married would celebrate many of the things they claim to believe in, faithfulness and honor and mutual caring under God."

Much as Lois and Mary would like to marry, however, they do not want what they call a "symbolic" marriage—neither the kind of ersatz ceremony Stephen and Ross had in 1981 in California, nor a ceremony presided over by a fully legitimate minister of an established religion who is willing to conduct such services even though it means going against the rules of his or her church. They want to be able to go down to city hall and get a license and have a religious ceremony that is approved by the religious hierarchy of that church and completely within its laws. We may be getting married when we're very old," Mary laughs. "But we still believe it will be possible eventually."

The great majority of gays and lesbians I interviewed for this book believe that "eventually" means decades, especially in terms of same-sex marriage becoming legal under the state and federal laws. Because an increasing number of ministers are challenging their own churches on the issue of same-sex marriage (a subject that will be discussed in detail in Chapter 7), many people expect religious ceremonies for same-sex couples to be approved, in at least a few denominations, within the next ten years, and quite possibly sooner. But few think that such unions will be the law of the land even by 2020. And it is the legal protections that would come with such a change that are most often given as the chief reason for supporting the concept of same-sex marriage in the first place. On other aspects of the subject, feelings are far more mixed.

Indeed, the majority of gays and lesbians appear to occupy a middle ground on the question of same-sex marriage. While they are for it on legal grounds, in that it would give gay and lesbian couples equality under the law with straight couples, and believe that such status would also mitigate against discrimination, attitudes in this very large middle group within the gay community are otherwise mixed, and sometimes uncertain. While some say they would take advantage of a change in the law, and marry their partners, others may not be so sure. A surprising number echo the arguments made by gays and lesbians on opposite sides of this issue. Thus, they would agree with Lois and Mary that the rights to marry, both legally and in a religious ceremony, should exist for gays, but in terms of their own personal lives find the idea a bit silly, backing Harris and Dale in this regard.

"Absolutely, gays and lesbians should be able to marry one another just as straight couples do. But would I do it? No way." This is Carl speaking. He is in his mid-thirties, a very successful businessman in Baltimore. "It's an important right in our society, and having it would go a long way toward giving us a kind of standing and respect we've never had. But—and it's a big but for me—the institution of marriage is pretty much in tatters even among straights. The 50-percent divorce rate, the number of people engaging in serial marriage, going through four or five spouses in a lifetime, all that, makes the very idea of marriage something of a joke in our society. Till our careers get in the way or I spot someone sexier is more like it than till death do us part.... And you know if they ever make same-sex marriage legal, it's going to make the whole idea even less appealing to everyone, straights and gays alike, if you ask me. It's like that old Groucho Marx joke about not wanting to belong to any club that would invite him to be a member. I have a couple of friends who want to get married, but I keep getting the feeling it's mostly because they can't. If they could, they wouldn't feel like second-class citizens, and there'd be less reason to get married in the first place. Of course these guys would do it, they'd have to or lose face, but a few years later they'd be going through a divorce. I'd bet on it."

Divorce. That isn't a subject that automatically comes up when gays and lesbians discuss same-sex marriage. And when the point is raised, a certain queasiness often sets in. As Stephen suggested, it's not a subject those who strongly favor same-sex marriage want to think about much. But if you ask any gay or lesbian with legal training about it, they can get quite snappish. Two different lawyers, one gay and one lesbian, used exactly the same words: "Anybody who thinks there's going to be legalized same-sex marriage without "divorce" laws kicking in, too, is plain dumb." In fact, nothing is so revelatory of the squishing thinking among many gays on this issue as introducing the word divorce into the discussion. It is also one of the main reasons why so many gays say the right should exist, but that they, personally, wouldn't exercise it.

One of the two lawyers quoted above is a woman who works as a senior aide to an important Democratic politician. She does not want to be identified beyond that, because of her concern that her own views could cause problems for her boss politically, right across the spectrum. "Nobody except for the lawyers working on specific cases," she says, "is being sufficiently hard-headed about same-sex marriage. On our side, I mean. Those who are unequivocally against it, and equate it with the collapse of civilization, know exactly where they stand and state their position very clearly. Most of them are bigots, of course, and their hatred and fear of homosexuality is emblazoned in their every statement. But they do have a well-constructed fortress to defend. On our side, we have a lot of guerilla bands that are attacking that fortress from several vantage points, but with far too little coordination. Some of them barely speak to one another."

She is willing to elaborate. "Andrew Sullivan deals very eloquently with same-sex marriage in his book *Virtually Normal.* As a lesbian I respond with a loud cheer to a great deal of what he has to say about the subject, especially in terms of how young gays would be helped by having role models who are partners in legal same-sex marriages. Of course, that would be an aid in dissipating some of the stigma against being gay. But as a lawyer, I can read some of the more intelligent conservative critiques of that book and say, 'I'm afraid you're right,' when they pick his logic apart. And frankly, if as brilliant a man as Andrew Sullivan can't write about same-sex marriage without contradicting himself by saying in one place that homosexuals are virtually like heterosexuals and then turning around and admitting they're different, who can? He leaves far too many holes for conservatives to drive right through. Everybody does."

The kinds of problems that this lesbian lawyer refers to are blatantly on display in the book *Same-Sex Marriage,* edited by Robert M. Bard and Stuart E. Rosenbaum. Diversity of opinion is built into this provocative selection of essays by both proponents and opponents of same-sex marriage. But while many of the essays championing same sex-marriage are eloquent and carefully argued, they end up undercutting one another since they approach the subject from so many different points of view. Experts from the fields of philosophy, psychology, religion, law, and social relations make their cases well enough when read individually, but when taken as a group they create confusion. So many different rationales are offered that to summarize the major points would result in a list that went on for pages. Subtle and complex reasoning does not get laws passed—simple, easily digested declarative statements, the fewer the better, result in legal changes. Ironically, the most direct, compact, and easily grasped essay in the book is *against* same sex marriage, written by the lesbian lawyer and activist, Paula L.

Ettelbrick, and called "Since When is Marriage a Path to Liberation?" She concludes, "We will be liberated only when we are respected and accepted for our differences and the diversity we provide to this society." Christine Pierce, a professor of philosophy, takes on Ettelbrick and other doubters, concluding that gay marriage "needs to be on the political agenda for the sake of gaining a certain level of social awareness and acceptance of serious lesbian and gay relationships."

The articles by Ettlebrick and Pierce put the differences between the gay separatists and the gay mainstreamers in a nutshell. One says that we must be respected even if we are different, the other that we can gain such respect only by demonstrating our ability to emulate the heterosexual family structure. Other writers, including Andrew Sullivan and Richard D. Mohr, go as far as to suggest that the legalization of same-sex marriages could give new vigor to the institution of marriage itself, for straights as well as gays. Ettlebrick has the perfect reply to such ideas in her very first sentence, in which she quotes a statement she saw on a t-shirt: "Marriage is a great institution. If you like living in institutions."

▼ ▼ ▼

Given the divisions within the gay community on the subject of same-sex marriage, it can seem surprising that the issue has become a front-burner one for many gay activists. The majority of gays and lesbians do appear to support same-sex marriages on the grounds that we should have the right to marry, but it is equally clear that the majority would not rush out to get a marriage license if it were possible to do so. Why then are some gay leaders expending so much energy in pursuing this change in the law? If they look behind them, they would have to wonder what happened to the footsoldiers that ought to be ranged behind their cavalry charge.

The answer to the why is a simple one. The majority of gays, regardless of whether they approve of marriage as an institution, are motivated by the fact that the heterosexual majority say we're not good enough, not moral enough, not mature enough to be allowed to marry. We're being treated like naughty children, and it grates. The passage of the Defense of Marriage Act by Congress, and it's signing by President Clinton, in 1996, did more to rally widespread gay and lesbian support for the right to marry than anything else. In sheer political terms, the act was a panicky reaction to the possibility that gay and lesbian marriages might be made legal in the State of Hawaii. The brief body of the act simply declares that no other "State, territory, or possession of the United States, or Indian tribe," will be required to recognize a same-sex marriage that was legal under the laws of any other state, territory, possession or tribe. But Congress then added insult to injury by amending the United States Code as follows:

> Section 7. Definition of "marriage" and "spouse"
> In determining the meaning of any Act of Congress, or of any ruling, regulation or interpretation of the various administrative bureaus and agencies of the United States, the word "marriage" means only a legal union between one man and one woman as husband and wife, and the word "spouse" refers to only a person of the opposite sex who is a husband or a wife.

So much for the long-term gay and lesbian couples who had been used to saying, "Oh, we're just as married as the Browns." Take that, you presumptuous misfits, our government was saying to us. It was not terribly surprising that the Republican-controlled Congress, dominated by right-wing zealots, should pass such an act, but the gay community was outraged that President Clinton would sign it. Despite the fact that he had appointed more than a hundred openly lesbian and gay officials throughout his administration, it seemed that once again he was prepared to desert us when the chips were down, just as he had in 1993 on the issue of gays in the military. Some gays just shrugged and said, "Well, it's an election year, what did you expect?" and gays voted for Clinton anyway in great numbers because he had done more for us than any other president. But there was real anger toward him even so.

Even some editorialists and commentators who had shown no particular inclination to support same-sex marriage were astounded by the sheer pettiness of the Defense of Marriage Act. Some conservatives were dismayed, because the title of act managed to suggest that marriage was in need of defending. In private conversation, some gays found it hilarious that it was deemed necessary to protect Native Americans, who had been treated like dirt for more than three centuries, from the ravages of gay marriages. But the chief effect of the act was to convince many gays and lesbians—many for the first time—that the right to marry was something they must have.

There are gays and lesbians, however, who have concluded, on reflection, that the Defense of Marriage Act could be construed as a kind of psychological victory for gay rights. One professor of American History said to me, "Overreaction by politicians has always been a sign of weakness. I don't think we'd have this act if the right wing wasn't frightened that it was losing the battle against ever-increasing rights and respect for gays and lesbians. And, as usually happens in these cases, passing the Defense of Marriage Act only succeeded in getting people who couldn't care less about same-sex marriage to support it more avidly. It reminds me of former President Cleveland's idiotic statement in 1905, 'Sensible and responsible women do not want to vote. The relative positions assumed by man and woman in the working out of our civilization were assigned long ago by a higher intelligence than ours.' Well, that just got a lot of 'sensible' women riled up who hadn't cared that much about the right to vote previously. And of course, that 'higher power' stuff figures in here too, even if it isn't explicitly stated in the language of the act. A colleague of mine, a woman with three kids and one of the best marriages I know, read the wording of the Defense of Marriage Act and said, 'Bill, I've just converted to supporting gay marriage.' The number of people who had that reaction may be small, but it is significant. And among gays, the act had a tremendous mobilizing effect."

Speaking in favor of the Defense of Marriage Act in the United States Senate, Jesse Helms, the right-wing firebrand from North

Carolina, resorted to an old joke that immediately raised the hackles of the gay community. He told of meeting a Baptist minister he knew in Washington just before the August recess. The minister, Helms recounted, suggested that he tell the folks back home in North Carolina that "God created Adam and Eve—not Adam and Steve." Unfortunately such low humor goes over well, not only with Helms's constituents in his home state but across the country. Gay marriage? What a joke. But his kind of cruelly humorous response to the issue masks real fear.

Richard D. Mohr puts his finger on the nature of that fear in his short essay, "The Stakes in the Gay Marriage Wars." He notes that during the hearings on the Defense of Marriage Act, the openly gay Representative Barney Frank of Massachusetts got the conservative Republican leader Henry Hyde of Illinois, a co-sponsor of the act, to admit that no heterosexual married couple would lose any material or legal right or benefit if same-sex marriage were allowed. But Hyde still balked at the idea because "It demeans the institution. The institution of marriage is demeaned by the same-sex marriage." Mohr notes that at that point we enter the "realm of cultural symbols." He goes on to say, "Marriage is the chief means by which culture maintains heterosexuality as a social identity. . . . One does not become heterosexual by having homosexual sex. Rather, marriage is the social essence of heterosexuality. And here's the kicker: if others were allowed to get married, one wouldn't be fully heterosexual either."

Many gays have a difficult time understanding the importance to heterosexuals of what Mohr is talking about. How many times have we said, on being told someone that we suspect of being gay is married, "Well, that doesn't mean anything." Most gays have been to bed with a married man at some point; a great many lesbians have been to bed with married women. We *know* that being married doesn't mean that someone is necessarily heterosexual, or at least not exclusively so. In addition, many gay men make an interesting judgement about straight men. If a straight man shows no reluctance whatsoever to hug an openly gay man, it is often taken as a sign of how secure he is with his heterosexuality. The married man who has absolutely no fear of embracing a gay man is seen as particularly straight. We tend to wonder about the supposedly straight man who is clearly nervous about physical contact with gay men. "What's he so worried about?" we ask. Here, I'm taking Mohr's idea a step further. For some married men, being married is a bulwark against their own sexual doubt. If gay men can be married too, that protection is gone.

Straight women are far more likely to admit that they have at one point or another felt a sexual attraction to another woman than straight men are to admit they ever have felt any such thing about a man. This suggests that future efforts to persuade the heterosexual majority that same-sex marriage should be allowed will be most effective with heterosexual women. My 1980 book, *Straight Women/Gay Men: A Special Relationship* explored in detail the fact that heterosexual women often find gay men to be particularly rewarding friends because such relationships involve neither the game playing likely to crop up with a heterosexual man nor the competitiveness that can exist between women. Such friendships also flourish because gay men tend to be far more sympathetic to feminist concerns than straight men. On one-hour long television show at the time the book came out, the host said to me, "You don't mean to say that straight men are out to keep both women and gay men in their places, are you?" He then cut directly into a commercial, obviously not wanting to hear an answer. Amusingly, when the show was over, he stalked into the dressing room to inform me that G. Gordy Liddy, of Watergate fame (and now a conservative radio host) was going to be on the next show. "Too bad he wasn't here today," my host said, "he probably would have punched you out." He then turned and walked out of the room. His producer, a woman, said, "Pay no attention to him. You did a great job and he knows it, that's why he's mad."

Same-sex marriage is something that straight women, twenty years later, are more prepared to deal with than straight men are. That gives gay and lesbian advocates of same-sex marriage an opening. Heterosexual opposition is far from monolithic. But the political process is still overwhelmingly dominated by men. That's why more than thirty states have passed measures to avoid recognition of same-sex marriages. Gays and lesbians do have their champions among male heterosexual politicians, more all the time and not just in states like New York and California where gays have a strong political clout. But the election of more women to political office would certainly help push a gay agenda, and same-sex marriage in particular, toward enactment more quickly.

As things stand, real movement is taking place only in the courts. That is, of course, a time honored path to social reform, one used to gain civil rights for black Americans and abortion rights for women. But the way the Baehr vs. Lewin case played out in Hawaii is not encouraging. After the Hawaii Supreme Court ruled in 1993 that it was unconstitutional to bar same-sex marriage under state law simply on the basis of gender, and sent the case back to the lower court, political pressure immediately began to build to find a way around the ruling. The legislature appointed a commission to study the matter; a majority found in favor of allowing same-sex marriages, but that conclusion was bitterly denounced in a minority report. The commission report was issued on December 8, 1995, and was followed almost exactly a year later by Circuit Court Judge Kevin Chang's ruling that the state of Hawaii could not forbid same-sex marriage.

In the meantime, however, the right wing had succeeded in getting the Defense of Marriage Act through congress. The Hawaii legislature, under terrific pressure, then passed an amendment to the state constitution specifically limiting marriage to male/female unions, an initiative ratified by the voters in 1998. In December of 1999, the state supreme court declared the issue moot because of the passage of the amendment—although the door to further legal action was left ajar in that the original finding that gays and lesbians were being discriminated against still stood.

Less than two weeks after the issue was declared moot in Hawaii, proponents of same-sex marriage were given new reason to hope when the Vermont Supreme Court stopped just short of of legalizing gay marriage. As in Hawaii, two lesbian couples, Stacy Jones and Nina Beck, and Lois Farnham and Holly Puterbaugh, were joined by a gay male couple, Peter Harrigan and Stan Baker, in suing the state for refusing them marriage licenses. In deciding the case, the Vermont Supreme

Court had Hawaii precedent to guide it, and gave the legislature less wriggle room. The legislature was instructed to do one of two things, either legalize same-sex marriage outright, or pass a domestic partnership law that would basically give same-sex couples all the legal protections afforded by marriage.

Proponents of same-sex marriage were elated. Legal experts noted that the Vermont state constitution was particularly difficult to amend, making it more difficult to stop gay marriage by the route taken in Hawaii (and also in Alaska, in a less publicized case). Following more than two months of emotional, but largely civil, debate on the subject throughout the state of Vermont, which indicated a deep split about how to proceed, a bill to create "civil unions" was approved in the Vermont House of Representatives on March 16, 2000, by a vote of 76 to 69. The Vermont Senate approved the bill, 19 to 11, on April 19; Democratic Governor Howard Dean had already agreed to sign it.; The bill did make a distinction between civil unions and marriages, but offered virtually the same rights to couples in same-sex unions as are available to married couples. Same-sex couples will apply for licences from town clerks, and be issued a certificate of union. They would then have all the rights and responsibilities that a married couple would under traditional law. Significantly, same-sex unions would also have to be dissolved in a family court if the partners separated—a "kind of divorce" to go with "a kind of marriage." Inevitably, those against any sort of legalized same-sex union were deeply upset, while those who had sought the right to actual marriage were also dismayed and promised to keep fighting.

Proponents of gay marriage are loath to say so, but the situation in Vermont holds some dangers for their cause. While there are many gays and lesbians for whom marriage itself is of supreme importance, the gay community as a whole might well be willing to settle for domestic partnership laws that would give gays and lesbians legal protections equal to those enjoyed by married straights. As noted throughout this chapter, there are many gays who back the idea of same-sex marriage primarily because of the legal protections it would provide. Gay separatists don't believe that even those legal considerations justify the embracing of what they consider a rigid and outmoded heterosexual tradition. What's more, domestic partnership laws that took care of the legal aspects of the matter might be far easier to pass in many other states, since they would not directly challenge the emotional symbolic meaning attached to the marriage between a man and a woman. To judge by his debate with Barney Frank, even a conservative like Representative Henry Hyde might be willing to go along with changes in domestic partnership law. They would not "demean" heterosexual marriage in the way he finds offensive.

Thus the gay community finds itself at a crossroad on this issue as the new century begins. There are those who deeply care about being married, in the full legal—and often religious—sense that heterosexuals are. But it is by no means clear that such individuals constitute a majority within the gay community. Many gays and lesbians I have talked to would be more than happy to settle for the kind of parity that could be established through revised domestic partnership laws. And if that is also a more attainable goal, they ask, why press for the right to marry? Why should this historic symbol of heterosexual union—so often used to keep women in their place—be so important to homosexuals if legal protections are equal for gay and lesbian partners?

It was only in the 1990s that gay marriage became a major issue. And it is an issue that has shown itself to be particularly troubling to the heterosexual majority, the kind of issue that seems to arouse greater opposition the closer it comes to reality. So long as certain controversial ideas remain "pie-in-the-sky" they can fly beneath the reactionary radar. But bring such an issue down to earth with an unexpected court victory, and that same idea will have every piece of available artillery turned upon it. The rejection of gay marriage in Hawaii and in Alaska was approved by two-thirds of the voters. And the idea upsets many heterosexuals to the degree that it could engender backlash against other important gay civil rights issues. Over the next several years the gay community as a whole is going to have to decide whether gay marriage is worth the fight. There are many indications that large numbers of gays and lesbians feel this issue may be carrying mainstreaming too far. Legal parity, yes. Marriage itself? What I have heard from many gays and lesbians is a resounding maybe.

five

Gay Adoption

Jon Holden and Michael Galluccio began living together in New York city in 1982 when they were still very young men. They later moved to New Jersey, and agreed to become foster parents to a boy named Adam, the son of a woman friend who was HIV-positive. Adam was three months old when they took him in. By the time he was two, they had decided to formally adopt him. Holden and Galluccio applied jointly to adopt Adam in March of 1995. After fifteen months they received a consent letter, but it bore only one of their names. The fine print of New Jersey law forbade joint adoptions by unmarried couples—heterosexual as well as homosexual. They would now have to start the expensive and lengthy process all over again, and the result, if approved, would have made them both parents of Adam, but still not technically joint parents. At this point, they turned to the ACLU for help, and suit was filed to overturn the New Jersey law.

In October of 1997, Judge Sybil R. Moses of the Superior Court in Bergen County handed down an opinion granting joint adoption on the grounds that it was best for the child. In December of 1997, a broader consent decree removed all legal barriers to joint adoption by unmarried couples, whether heterosexual or homosexual. New Jersey thus became the first state in the unions to treat all adoptions alike, whether the couple applying was unmarried or married, a male/female couple or a same-sex couple. Holden and Galluccio became instant heroes to those in the gay community who were fighting to gain equality under the law in adoption procedures across the country. With their success came media attention from major magazines and newspapers as well as from gay publications and legal journals. It also brought attacks from such organizations as the Family Research Council, founded by the Republican presidential candidate Gary Bauer and heavily funded by the Religious Right.

Holden and Galluccio, now 34 and 36, were able to handle this media onslaught with grace. But it also pushed them into a kind of openness that neither had originally contemplated. As Michael Galluccio told the *Advocate* in the spring of 1999, "I can't tell you how many times I've been at ShopRite with Adam in the shopping cart and someone will say, 'Is it Mommy's day off?' and I will respond, 'There is no mom. Adam has another dad.'" To take things a step further, Jon Holden legally changed his name to Jon Holden-Galluccio on their sixteenth anniversary in 1997. In June 1998, the Galluccios were united in a "holy union" at an Episcopal church on Father's day. Although this marriage does not have legal standing, it served to complete the journey they had begun when they took Adam in. The previous month they had completed the adoption of a second foster child, Madison, and are planning to adopt his 16 year old step-sister Rosa as well.

Adoption in the United States is covered by state law, and the statutes differ widely from state to state even for married couples. Florida, which is infamous for its over zealous foster care agencies even in seemingly straight forward situations, is the only remaining state that has a specific law banning adoptions for gays or lesbians, but that is being fought county by county by the ACLU. New Hampshire also had a law banning adoptions by gays and lesbians, but it was finally rescinded on May 3, 1999, when Governor Jeanne Shaheen signed a bill ending such discrimination. But this action, like the New Jersey consent decree, only intensified the anti-gay efforts of the Religious Right in regard to adoption.

In 1999 alone, attempts to ban gays and lesbians from adopting children were introduced—either as legislative bills or as campaigns for ballot referendums—in Idaho, Indiana, Oklahoma, Texas, and Utah. Measures of the same sort were defeated in Arizona, California, Georgia, and Missouri in 1998, but efforts to reintroduce them are widely expected. Sometimes a state agency, whether on its own initiative or in response to anti-gay pressure, institute an ad hoc rule without benefit of a legislative bill or ballot referendum. One such rule is being challenged in Arkansas by the ACLU. There the Child Welfare Agency Review Board passed a new policy in January of 1999 that not only cut off the possibility of adoption by gays and lesbians, but even by heterosexuals who happen to live with someone gay.

Conservatives in Congress often inveigh against gay and lesbian adoptions, as they do against same-sex marriage. The Defense of Marriage Act, discussed in the previous chapter, was an attempt to contain the burgeoning movement for same-sex marriage in several states. On the adoption front, the House of Representatives passed a measure banning gay and lesbian adoptions in Washington, D.C., for which Congress has oversight power. This bill, introduced by a leading "family values" stalwart, Republican representative Steve Largent of Oklahoma, was passed by a 227 to 192 vote in September of 1998, when the Republican majority in the House was larger than it would be following the elections that November. The measure died in the Senate, but it's passage by the House indicates the strength of the anti-gay forces in the Republican party.

But despite the ominous meddling by the House and, on the state level, the advances for gay adoptions in New Jersey and New Hampshire, such battles are often fought out at the local level. Going back to the 1980s, courts in the liberal San Francisco area have often allowed gay and lesbian adoptions to proceed, regardless of what was going on in the rest of the State of California. But while there have been numerous victories at the local level over the years, some of the most troubling cases have developed because a single bureaucrat has taken an anti-gay stand that has thrown the lives of gay or lesbian parents into turmoil.

For example, in 1997 an Austin, Texas, child-welfare worker discovered that her agency had placed a foster child in the home of a lesbian who had a live-in partner. Rebecca Bledsoe immediately ordered the child removed. Her reasoning was that homosexual activity remains illegal in Texas in principal if not in terms of enforcement, and that went against the rule that a child should never be placed in an environment where criminal activity was known to exist. Fortunately, Bledsoe's superiors at Austin's Child Protection Services stepped in and restored the child to the lesbian foster parent. Because Bledsoe overstepped her authority by removing a child from an approved home without any emergency that suggested the child was at immediate risk, she was demoted. Beldsoe protested, the case became public, and anti-gay conservatives championed her as a heroine.

The furor that resulted in Texas has ramifications that continue to this day. Bills were introduced in the Texas legislature to ban gays and lesbians from becoming foster or adoptive parents. In January of 1999, the right-wing Family Research Council singled out another lesbian couple who were in the process of adopting twins born to a Texas woman that month. A letter from the Family Research Council was sent to all Texas legislators, trying to drum up support for a bill outlawing gay parenting and naming the couple adopting the twins, Elizabeth Birch and Hilary Rosen. These two women are prominent people. Birch serves as executive director of America's largest gay rights organization, the Human Rights Campaign, based in Washington, D.C., while Rosen is president of the recording industry's trade and lobbying group in Washington, the Recording Industry Association of America. The adoption went through, but as an article in the *Advocate* pointed out, "the fear it caused the couple was familiar to millions of gay parents across America who seek legal and social recognition for their children. If Birch and Rosen—well-connected Washington power-brokers—could be threatened with losing a child, it could happen to anyone."

In its letter to Texas legislators, the Family Research Council hit in a familiar theme, saying that the twins Brich and Rosen had arranged to adopt at birth would be better served by being placed in a "traditional family." This is, of course, the standard rallying cry of the religious right. But the council may not have been aware of quite how that phrase would echo in the ears of those versed in arguments about adoption that have been raging for the past thirty years. The fact is that—leaving gay and lesbian adoptions completely aside—this whole subject is rife with controversy.

As it happens, I am myself an adopted child, and thus have a natural long-standing interest in the subject. My parents were married in their mid-thirties at the height of the Great Depression in 1933. My father had fought in Europe in the last days of World War I, graduated from Emory University, and then joined a major stove-manufacturing company in Cleveland, Tennessee. By his late twenties he had decided that he would rather teach than remain in business, took a master's degree at the University of Virginia and then went on to Princeton for his Ph.D. While at Princeton, he met my mother, who was teaching at Miss Fine's School. My mother was thirty-five when she first became pregnant and had a miscarriage that nearly took her life. A decision was made to adopt, and I was chosen from the Home of Little Wanderers (the first adoption agency in the country, founded during the Civil War) in New Haven, Connecticut, while my father was teaching at Hotchkiss, the prep school. That was in 1939. It was a closed adoption (the name of my birth mother was known only to the agency). I was not quite a year old when I was adopted, and by that time my father had begun teaching at Phillips Academy, Andover, on whose campus I grew up.

Over the years, I met many other adopted children. There were several others at the school, and four years later my parents adopted my sister, Heath. Later I would encounter many other adoptees—we tend to find each other. I grew up in a "traditional family," as did most of the adopted children I knew. My parents were not particularly religious and were quite liberal in their politics—neither of which would please the Family Research Council, pointing up how narrow its definitions actually are. More specifically, my own experience of being an adopted child, and my friendship with many others, is at odds with many things that the religious right believes to be true about "family values."

I had an extraordinarily rich and warm relationship with my parents. I cannot remember not knowing that I was adopted—they started telling me very early. Yet I have know adopted children who disliked their parents—just as I have known many genetic children who couldn't stand theirs. It is my opinion, and that of the vast majority of adopted children I have known, that whether you are an adopted or genetic child has almost nothing to do with how your relationship with your parents turn out. It is perfectly possible that a genetic child will turn out to have a personality very similar to that of Aunt Sophie or Uncle Charlie, and if that child's parents can't stand Sophie or Charlie, the relationship with their own offspring is likely to be a difficult one. An adopted child, on the other hand, may turn out to have a personality and range of interests that is almost perfectly congruent with the adoptive parents. That was true in my case; it was not in my sister's. To a degree, the child/parent relationship is always something of a roulette game, whether the child is genetic or adopted. An adult of either sex, married or unmarried, straight or gay, conservative or liberal, religious or not, may turn out to be an excellent parent for one child and a lousy parent for another child. Look around you; the evidence is everywhere.

One of the nastier insinuations made by the right-wingers against gay parents is that any child they adopt is at risk of becoming gay also. Never mind, at this juncture, that the vast majority of medical and psychological professionals agree that children are born gay or straight, and have no choice whatsoever their sexual orientation. Let's simply turn around the proposition that gay parents are likely to "influence" their child's sexual orientation. If that were true, why aren't I straight? The parents who adopted me certainly were. How come they weren't able to instill me with heterosexual desires? Does the right wing believe that the heterosexual example is less powerful than the gay example? What fun it would be to get them to admit that!

But my own experience with being an adopted child, knowing many others, and following the subject with interest most of my life also raises other issues. There have been fierce arguments among adoption officials and experts for years about the correct placement of children even within "traditional" households. There are those who insist that a child should always be placed with adoptive parents of the same race or the same religious faith as the birth mother. This was a major issue during the 1980s in regard to the placement of black children and those from foreign countries.

These racial and religious issues remain contentious in some quarters, but those who say that a good home is a good home have been winning largely by default. There are too many children without parents to indulge in the luxury of matching race and religion. But it needs to be understood by gays and lesbians seeking to adopt children that the anti-gay forces have allies within the hierarchy of adoption officials and agencies, whether public or private. Someone who does not like the idea of having a black baby being placed with a white family is all too likely to see a procedural advantage in siding with the anti-gay forces. That is why gays and lesbians seeking to adopt may find to their surprise that they are fighting not only anti-gay forces but also sometimes people who would not seem to have a stake in that particular debate.

This is not to play down the sheer anti-gay bigotry involved, but merely to note that the problem can be more complex than it seems on the surface. There are numerous different routes to adoption, each with its pluses and minuses. The most difficult for prospective gay and lesbian parents is adoption through an established, state-licensed adoption agency, whether public or private. In many states, the rules and regulations covering such adoptions are onerous to the point that even married heterosexual couples with a spotless background and substantial income may have to wait as long as two years for an available child. In addition, any blemish discovered in background checks—and most people have some past or current problems—can derail the entire process. The literature on adoption, from popular books to academic studies, is full of horror stories to go along with the many success stories. Given the time and legal obstacles involved, most gays and lesbians seek out alternative avenues to adoption.

So-called "open adoptions," in which the adoptive parents and the birth mother are fully known to one another, and in most cases actually meet, present other difficulties. As the acclaimed 1997 television movie *The Baby Dance* documents, an open adoption can lead to emotional confrontations between the birth mother (and in the case of this story, the father as well) and the adoptive parents, and can end badly all around, even when married heterosexual couples are involved. Open adoptions almost always call for the adoptive parents to pay thousands of dollars in pre-natal care, living expenses, and medical bills to the birth mother. In many cases such arrangements give the birth mother (and occasionally the father) visitation rights as well. Open adoptions are controversial even among adoption professionals, for reasons ranging from ethical considerations to the well-being of the child. They can be very expensive, since there are inevitably hefty lawyers' fees to deal with in addition to the payments made to the birth mother. For gays and lesbians wishing to adopt, an open adoption can work only if the birth mother is completely comfortable with having the child she has carried to term raised by gay or lesbian parents.

The adoption of foreign children is increasingly common for gays and lesbians, as it is among heterosexual couples. Experts are hard put to come up with solid figures about foreign adoptions, but some have hazarded a guess that as many as 80 percent of gay and lesbian adoptions are of foreign children. Here again, expenses are high, an adoption can fall through at the last moment, and, in some cases, the baby has subsequently been found to have a physical or mental problem. Gays and lesbians who have adopted foreign children are seldom willing to speak for the record on the subject, for fear that officials in the United States or even in the country from which the child was adopted might cause problems if the fact that the adoptive parents are gay or lesbian were to emerge.

Some gays and lesbians have adopted children whom they originally took in as a foster child, as was the case with Jon Holden-Galluccio and Michael Galluccio in New Jersey. In states with fairly liberal laws, public welfare departments have sufficient need to find foster parents that a gay or lesbian has a reasonable chance to be fairly considered. And once a child has spent a year or two with a foster parent, and the situation has worked well, state agencies and the courts are often willing to look with favor on a subsequent application to adopt the child, on the grounds that a stable environment is of primary importance for that child. But there are no guarantees, and a foster parent seeking to adopt must be able to live with the idea that they could lose all contact with a child they have come to love.

A few gays and lesbians have come up with novel solutions to the desire to have a child. A heterosexual woman I know agreed to be artificially inseminated with the sperm of a gay friend. She is a photographer who travels the globe constantly, and although she did not want to raise a child, she did want to have the experience of bearing one. The adoption was arranged with no problems in the San Francisco area; the gay man had a daughter to raise and the woman had the biological experience she wanted. More often, this kind of arrangement is reversed, with a lesbian finding a sperm donor of her choice and then raising the child. A couple I knew well in the 1970s reached an even more complex agreement. The woman couldn't stand sex—with man or woman. She married a gay man and was artificially inseminated with his sperm. They remained married until their son was two years old and then filed for the amicable divorce planned from the start. Their son was raised by the woman, but saw his father on a regular basis. The father soon began living with a long-term male partner, whom the boy called by his first name, but came to consider "a second father." The son is now twenty-five, married and the father of a son of his own. What's more, father, mother, dad's lover, son, and son's wife are all regular church-goers. It's enough to give the Family Research Council apoplexy.

Beyond the question of seeking a child to adopt—or finding creative ways around it—the fact of life for some gay men and many lesbians is the existence of genetic children conceived in a marriage that was originally entirely genuine but later ended in divorce. There are many individuals of both sexes who do not fully recognize, or at least admit, their true sexual orientation until their thirties or even later. By that time they may have a child or even several children. Provided the heterosexual spouse does not make trouble by seeking sole custody on the grounds that their former husband or wife is homosexual, the children often end up being raised by the gay or lesbian parent. That is particularly true for lesbians, since the legal system, and our society as a whole, tends to the belief that a child is better off with the mother unless she has a serious problem such as drug abuse, alcoholism, or abusive tendencies. In many such cases, the gay or lesbian parent who has primary care of a child will find a long-term same-sex partner, and in time that partner may want to make the new family unit official by adopting the partner's genetic child.

The reasons for taking such a step can range from the emotional to the very practical. In legal terms, these are known as "second parent adoptions." The concept of second parent adoptions was developed in the 1980s by what was then called the Lesbian Rights Project and is now known as the National Center for Lesbian Rights. The concept played an important part in lower court decisions in San Francisco during that period, when the first such adoptions were permitted.

The history and legal ramifications of these adoptions were detailed in an article by Jeffrey G. Gibson, a San Francisco attorney in *Human Rights: Journal of Individual Rights and Responsibilities,* in the Spring 1999 issue. The article was published in connection with the adoption of a resolution by the American Bar Association on February 8, 1999: "RESOLVED, that the American Bar Association supports the enactment of laws and implementation of public policy that provide that sexual orientation shall not be a bar to adoption when the adoption is determined to be in the best interest of the child."

The support of the ABA on this issue is important because courts at all levels across the country are currently deciding second parent adoption cases, and are forced to do so in the context of laws that make such adoptions difficult. Privately executed legal documents such as wills and guardianship agreements offer some protection for the child of one gay or lesbian partner if he or she should become incapacitated or die, by nominating the surviving partner as the child's primary caregiver. But the courts do not have to accept such nominations and have the power to remove the child to the care of another interested party, such as a grandmother, or even to give the child over to foster care. Only legal adoption of the child by the partner can ensure that the child will remain with the partner. That may be what the child wants, and may be best for the child, but the Christian right has made a habit of challenging such outcomes in recent years when only a will or guardianship agreement is in place.

Without formal adoption procedures, even a smaller crisis can turn into a nightmare. A same-sex partner may not be accepted as having the authority to approve an emergency operation such as an appendectomy for a child. At hospitals where the "next of kin" rule is rigidly enforced, a same-sex partner may not even be permitted to visit the child. Problems could also develop if the biological parent was away and the child got into trouble at school or with the police. A child could be packed off to a shelter rather than being released into the custody of the same-sex partner. And while many officials are willing to be both humane and practical in such crisis, there are always those "go by the book" individuals who will not bend to common sense.

It should be noted that these same problems can develop for unmarried heterosexual partners. This is an area where the rights of unmarried opposite-sex partners and same-sex partners overlap. But the opposite-sex partners can marry, while the same-sex members cannot. For same-sex partners, that leads to a Catch-22 that can render any attempt at adoption absurd. As Jeffrey G. Gibson explains, "Most state adoption statutes provide that a biological parent who consents to the adoption of a child must give up or "cut off" his or her own parental rights, unless the adopting party is the parent's legal spouse and thus a stepparent to the child. Given that no state currently permits same-sex couples to marry, the key legal question for the courts ruling on second parent adoptions has been whether to forego an overly literal and rigid interpretation of state adoption statutes in order to advance the statute's underlying purpose of promoting the child's best interests."

This Catch-22 means, in essence, that the judge in the case must be willing to be creative in his or her interpretation of the law—the very thing that conservative politicians and the judges they appoint rail against. The majority of judges in the country at present are conservatives, and even in jurisdictions known for their liberalism, conservative judges—or judges who are biased against homosexuality—do crop up. Nevertheless, progress has been made on this issue. In three states, cases involving same-sex adoptions have been decided at the state supreme court level that permit the partner to adopt without the biological parent giving up his or her rights. Those states are Massachusetts, New York, and Vermont. Second parent adoptions have been permitted by intermediate appellate courts in Connecticut, the District of Columbia, Illinois, and New Jersey. Lower Courts in have approved such adoptions in another fifteen states, but at this level the picture becomes more confused. In my own state of Pennsylvania, lower court decisions have gone both ways, and the issue will have to be decided at higher levels. Lower courts in Texas have permitted second parent adoptions, but that has only given impetus to the efforts of state legislators to put a stop to the practice. And while California led the way on this issue in the San Francisco area, that spurred then governor Pete Wilson to try to stop same-sex adoptions with an administrative proposal in 1996, the final year of his second term. He was thwarted, but California remains a hotbed of anti-gay bills and referendums on this and other gay rights issues. The situation in Texas and California underline the fact that when gay rights make progress on any new front, reactionary forces often begin gearing up to fight those advances.

The gay community itself is far from unanimously behind the campaign for same-sex adoption rights. Many gays and some lesbians express reservations about the new emphasis on this issue, and a few are strongly against it. The reasons for such doubts range from political practicality to ideological principle, with a considerable measure of personal prejudices added to the mix.

As in the case of gay marriage, there are some gays who turn derisive at the mere mention of same-sex adoption. "Here we go again," says Bobby, thirty-two, who manages a gay bookstore. "Tom and Jerry spend ten years getting up the nerve to come out, and then they turn around and want to marry each other and adopt children. They've been so brainwashed by the straight society that they can't stand being gay. They have to prove that even though they want to suck each other's dicks, they're really just 'normal' guys who can't wait to buy a crib and really look forward to car-pooling. This is just the old guilt reasserting itself, if you ask me. And of course it helps them get back in their parents' good graces. Mom and Dad may have turned pale when Tom told them he was gay, but what do you know, he's going to give them grandchildren after all, even if they are going to be raised by two faggots. Hurrah, hurrah, the family will go on! It makes me want to throw up."

When these comments were repeated to Frank, thirty-four, a tax attorney who adopted a girl from an Eastern European country in 1997, he laughed and said, "Here we go again indeed. I don't know what's worse, being stereotyped by straights or by other gays. I came out to my family when I was nineteen, and my parents hardly blinked. A couple of relatives were aghast, but they were aghast about almost everything. I didn't adopt a child to please my parents, and I don't have any guilt about being gay. It's just a fact of life to me. I've always liked kids, I think they enrich one's life enormously, and after Sam and I had been together eight years, we thought it was time to start a family. We're already involved in trying to adopt another kid, hopefully a boy. Sam will be the legal father this time. The problems with joint adoption were too complicated to deal with, but things are changing, and we hope we'll be able to adopt one another's kids down the line. Maybe we'll move to New Jersey, since you can do it there now. Of course there are gays who aren't going to want to adopt kids, maybe the majority feel that way, but they shouldn't tell those of us who want children how to feel and think. Homosexuals are just as diverse as heterosexuals—how many times does that need to be said?"

Setting up a long-distance debate, I told Bobby about Frank's response to his original comments. "I don't deny there are all kinds of gays. Since I don't know Frank, it's tough to say exactly what's going on, but I still think there's a brainwashing effect involved. You have to have children to be conventional in this society. You're out of it in a way if you don't. With women maybe it's different, maybe there's some sort of inborn 'maternal instinct,' but I even wonder about that. I know several straight women who never wanted kids, can't stand them in fact. What's that great line by Florence King about sexual abuse of children, how she could never understand it because to have sexual contact with a child, you'd have to actually spend time in the same room with them. I know lots of women—straight and lesbian—who feel exactly that way. If somebody really wants a kid, despite being gay, fine, whatever makes you happy. But why do people want them? Is that nature or what our society says you should feel? It really is a question, and not just for gays. There are millions of people who shouldn't have kids, they'd make a complete mess of it. My parents for example. And, yes, I am fully aware that just gives ammunition to the other side. I had an unhappy childhood, so I am soured on the whole deal. That may be true. But it also may be true that the ones who want kids have been brainwashed. That's the trouble with psychology, isn't it, it's always so much easier to figure out what makes the other person tick?"

The fact that there are numerous schools of psychology that expend a great deal of energy trying to blow one another out of the water suggests that answers to questions of motivation and conditioning are somewhat less than universal under any circumstances, and almost beside the point in discussing an issue as complex as same-sex adoption. Some gays and lesbians want very much to have children; others disdain the very idea. But there are concerns of a less personal nature that have been raised by the new emphasis on the issue.

Michael Bronski, author of *The Pleasure Principle: Sex, Backlash, and the Struggle for Gay Freedom* is concerned about the trend to gay adoption, because, he told the *Advocate,* "gay parenting may drain energy from the grass roots politics." Bronski notes that urban areas have always been the "heart and soul of gay life," and feels that as gay parents move to the suburbs to raise children, the pool of activists willing to do the in-the-trenches work is dwindling. Certainly it is true that state and municipal laws, school board regulations, employment rules in a vast majority of businesses, and numerous other bureaucratic strictures make life difficult for gays and lesbians. The fight to get such laws and regulations changed is an inch-by-inch one that requires tireless efforts, and there are few enough activists on the front lines as it is.

But the suspicion among many gays, including Bronski, that gay parenting is almost invariably accompanied by a withdrawal from activism appears to be contradicted by at least some high profile cases. It was, after all, exactly because of their desire to jointly adopt their son Adam that the Galluccios embarked on a course that led to the overhaul of New Jersey adoption regulations. The Galluccios have specifically said that what they had to go through in pressing their cases forced them to become more open than they had ever expected to be. It was not while living in their New York City apartment in the earlier years of their relationship that they crusaded for a basic gay right, but out of their home in the suburb of Maplewood, New Jersey. It was gay parenting that turned them into activists.

Moreover, many gay and lesbian parents have realized that adoption regulations are tied up with much broader issues. Mary, thirty-five, and her partner Sandra, thirty-three, were both married previously, and each has a child under ten from that marriage. They live in a Southern state, and in 1995 they suddenly realized that they were vulnerable in a way they hadn't previously considered. "I remember reading about the case of Sharon Bottoms in the newspapers," Mary says. "There she was, the natural mother of a two-year-old, but living with a lesbian partner. And the state of Virginia took her son sway from her and gave custody to her mother because she had been ruled an unfit mother under the state sodomy law. Her own baby! And I said to Sandra, 'My God, there's a sodomy law on the books here too. They could take our own kids away from us!' We were just petrified! Now, nobody has been prosecuted under the state sodomy law for some time, and some of my gay friends said that if that happened, it was more likely to be a man they'd go after. But it was scary even so. All you would need would be some right-wing neighbor with clout to get the Christian right all stirred up, and you'd find yourself fighting to keep your own kid. Sandra and I looked into things further, and we found out there were a great many states with sodomy laws still in place, and they were being used all over the country to prevent gays and lesbians from adopting. The Virginia case was unusual, true, in that Sharon Bottoms' mother started this whole mess, and other places weren't taking biological kids away from their mothers, just keeping gay and lesbians from adopting. But we started sending contributions to organizations that were fighting those laws. We're still doing it. We're not front-line activists because we don't want to put ourselves or our kids in harm's way. But we are doing something to help, and before we heard about Sharon Bottoms we weren't doing anything."

There are gay and lesbian parents all across the country who are doing the same thing as Mary and Sandra, lending financial support but keeping their heads down, at least if they live in a state where the sodomy laws are tied to definitions of a "fit parent." The fear of being targeted by anti-gay organizations does appear in this sense to deter upfront activism by many gay and lesbian parents. But anecdotal reports do suggest that few of these people were activists before they were parents—giving money is a step toward activism for such individuals. At the same time, however, the caution about protesting openly against sodomy laws—leaving the battle to those who are less vulnerable to retaliation—leads to another reason why some gays and lesbians are less than fully supportive of gay and lesbian adoption.

"It's asking for trouble," says Donald, a professor of sociology at a state-funded university in New York. Donald, like may educators, especially in publicly funded institutions, is out, but not out. He and his lover march on gay pride day, and they are fairly conspicuous since Donald is white and his lover is black. Donald hates the word "partner," which is interesting considering his situation. "Reggie and I are lovers, that's for sure. We're friends unquestionably. We're housemates, obviously, since we live together. But partners? We really laughed, and nudged one another when we went to see *American Beauty,* and two gay men in the neighborhood introduced themselves to the Marine officer as partners, and the middle-aged Marine assumes they're in the same business. It's even better, of course, that the Marine turns out to be the most closeted man in the Western world."

While Donald and Reggie are marching in the gay pride parade, the rainbow banner is hanging in the front of their home, although they wonder sometimes how many of their neighbors understand its significance. Donald thinks that all his colleagues at the university are aware he's gay, but with most of them it is not discussed. "They don't care that I'm gay," he says, "but aside from the dozen or so other gays on the faculty, not caring also means not caring to talk about it. And I think that's true for most straights. That's where the problem lies for pushing the envelope on gay adoption and gay marriage. Tolerance is an interesting word. It's often used these days as though it were some cardinal virtue. If everyone was tolerant of everyone else, there'll be fewer problems, the politicians say. But tolerance in that usage is kind of thin ice, it seems to me. Let's remember the far more established uses of the word. 'I can tolerate a good deal of pain.' Or, 'I can tolerate opera once in a while.' A good deal of pain. Once in a while. In other words, tolerance has its limits. I think we've just reached a point where the majority of the public can tolerate gays. But now we're going to stuff gay adoption and gay marriage down their throats? I worry, and I worry a lot, that a whole lot of people are going to say, 'Enough already. That's intolerable.'"

Donald is a liberal politically, but a man of moderation in most other ways. He is not against gay adoption or gay marriage per se. Yet even though he understands that adoption laws need to be changed to protect the relationships of gays and, particularly, lesbians with the children they already have, he doesn't think the general public is ready to accept gay adoption as a "norm." He is horrified by what happened to Sharon Bottoms in Virginia, and supports unreservedly the repeal of the sodomy laws that were at the root of her problems. "Trying to separate a child from a parent who is homosexual is bigotry raised to a criminal level," he says. In addition he is perfectly willing to understand that not only lesbians but some gay men may sincerely want to have children; he is not a gay separatist who believes that gays having children amounts to nothing more than a parody of the straight life. But he thinks it is too soon to press so hard on this issue, and that to do so may lead to a broader backlash against gays. Asked when the general public may be ready, ten years, twenty years, he replies, "Ten would be nice. But let's get rid of the sodomy laws and consolidate our gains on things like health insurance for gay partners first."

Donald's caution on this issue is more widely shared by "third way" gays than may be realized by gay activists and those caught up in adoption battles. Many gays I have talked to share Donald's view that things are moving too fast on this front for the gay community in general. Same-sex adoption is more widely favored by lesbians, as might be expected, since there are large numbers of lesbian moms. But even among lesbians, there are those who worry. Laura is social worker, and although she is strongly in favor of same-sex adoption in principle, she says that it is a subject that makes a lot of straight people angrier than may be recognized by gay activists. "I hear it all the time," she says, "and it's not put politely. It's 'who do these faggots think they are?' I hear it from co-workers, women with kids of their own. I hear it from my clients. They're not saying it to me, it's stuff I overhear. That may be an ironic thing to hear from a nineteen-year-old unmarried woman barely out of her teens with three children by three different men, but it's there. You can call it ignorance or sheer bigotry, but that won't make it go away. It's even more unnerving when I get it from my middle-class co-workers, women who are in professions that demand empathy for others. Most of them do have sympathy for women who got married, had a child and then decided they had to live as lesbians. But gay men adopting children? They can get vicious about that. I have an old friend, going back to high school. She was the first person I came out to, and we're still close. She's got two kids and she says she hears other mothers—upper-middle-class, educated, full of good works—who don't like the idea at all, either. She says many of them don't think much of the fathering instincts of straight men, sometimes including their own husbands. Gay men? Forget it."

Suspicions about the parenting skills of a gay man or lesbian can be countered. An oft-cited survey published by *Child Development* in 1992 looked at thirty studies of children raised by gay or lesbian parents. Almost without exception, these studies concluded that the children of gay and lesbian parents had developed as normally as the children of married straight couples. There is of course a study funded by the Family Research Institute, conducted by a well-known anti-gay researcher, Paul Cameron, that comes to the opposite conclusion, but it has been widely discredited by child development professionals on the basis of both its methodology and the known bias of its author.

I know a number of gay and lesbian parents myself, and for what it's worth, their children seem as well adjusted as anyone else's. There are a couple of kids with problems, but then I know plenty of kids from "traditional" families who have problems. An old friend from college presents a particularly interesting case. He got divorced and came out when his sons were ten and thirteen. Not only was he awarded custody, but that was what his sons wanted. Now grown, they are clearly proud of their father, and very close to him, and have no doubts about their own heterosexuality. The son of another friend was brought up by his mother after his parents were divorced, but the son visited his father regularly. The father has lived with the same male partner for the past fourteen years. Soon after his son got out of the Marines, he visited his dad and a few weeks later called him up and said, "I just wanted to tell you, Dad, that I am proud of you. I guess you know that, but I thought maybe it was time to say it out loud." The son got married a year later, in a small civil ceremony, and brought his new bride to visit his father and partner a few weeks later. Such stories abound, and while they cannot stand as clinical evidence of the ability of children to not only develop normally but to have real respect for gay parents, they do bear repeating.

The anti-gay right wing, of course, doesn't want to hear such stories, and inevitably discounts them. The right wing is on the lookout for horror stories, and unsurprisingly, they occasionally find one. I know a woman whose son was pushed down a flight of stairs when he discovered that she had come out as a lesbian after her much older husband's death. The son, then in his twenties, simply could not deal with this revelation at the time, but his mother and lesbian partner of a dozen years are now regularly invited to visit the son, his wife and their five children. I once asked my friend if she thought her son was trying to prove something by having so many children. She smiled and said with great calm, "Obviously."

The broader public seems to believe both kinds of stories, the heartwarming ones about closeness between grown children and their gay parents, and the occasional horror story. In doing so, they exhibit a common-sense understanding that family relationships are complex and that problems can arise even in the "best families." There is also the fact that "traditional" families, Mom, Pop, two kids, a dog or a cat, and living in the same place until you go away to college or get a job, are less and less common. The divorce rate, the ever-growing number of single parents, the deracination that pervades our extremely mobile society, all announce that Ozzie and Harriet are an endangered species, even as a semi-fake ideal. People know that, and many gay and lesbian leaders on the same-sex adoption front point to that fact as being helpful in fighting to make gay adoption an accepted legal fact throughout the country.

Maybe. Yet there is clear evidence in poll after poll that Americans are not happy about the transformations that are taking place. The lack of "moral fiber" in the country is regularly at the top of the list among things Americans worry most about. And that concern is clearly linked with the so-called "breakdown of the traditional family." That may be the reason why the polls continue to show the public rejecting the idea of gay adoption by considerable margins. A June 1997 poll conducted by Princeton Survey Research Associates for the Pew Research Center found that 56 percent thought that homosexual couples raising children was a "bad thing." Only 6 percent thought it was a good thing, but in a more heartening figure, 31 percent thought it made no difference. An additional 7 percent said they didn't know. Gay and lesbian activists will say that these results mean we only have to change the minds of 14 percent of the population to gain a majority that either thinks homosexual parenting is a good thing or at least makes no difference. But this is not an election poll, where one candidate can make a mistake and another surge forward in the space of a few weeks. This is a poll of basic world views. These take much longer to change, historically.

With the American Bar Association now behind the push for legal equality for same-sex adoptions, it is not unreasonable to hope that things will move faster. For the most part, the gay and lesbian leaders who are pressing for such change are eminently responsible people. There are few radical protest types involved in promoting same-sex adoption—in fact, most radicals appear to be against the gay adoption agenda, because it is alien to their interest in promoting the gay lifestyle as a separate way of being. Indeed, many gay radicals aren't interested enough in same-sex adoption to spend much time on the subject aside from issuing the occasional withering comment. Thus the fight for same-sex adoption can proceed in a way that is not likely to cause backlash because of public disruptions that make the evening news.

On the other hand, a surprising number of sober-minded gays, and some lesbians, even when they approve in principle of same-sex adoption, are worried that a backlash will arise simply because the subject is too volatile, and feeds into too many other concerns that the broad public has about the moral status of the country. Such fears may be just fears. Some older gays who remember all too well what it was like in the pre-Stonewall days will even admit that their nervousness may simply be a holdover from another time. But there are younger people in the gay community who are wary, too. Too many teenagers still hear "faggot" muttered in school corridors for even younger people to be certain that things have changed as much as big-city anti-discrimination laws or increasing corporate willingness to institute health plans that cover same-sex partners might indicate.

There is no question that the issue of same-sex adoption arouses the right wing to action. Every step forward is met by more strident attacks, not only verbally, but in terms of bringing legal actions and promoting legislative and anti-gay measures. There are gay leaders who believe that the right-wing counterattack plays into the hands of gay adoption advocates. Despite the personal attacks by the right wing in her own adoption case, Human Rights Campaign director Elizabeth Birch told the *Advocate,* "Americans are very reluctant to interfere in personal decisions about parenting. They don't want the religious right making any decision for them." Birch may be correct in assuming that the right wing is going too far in combating same-sex adoption, and will drive more straights to side with gays and lesbians on the issue, but there are beginning to be signs that the right wing is realizing that it is dangerous to appear too strident—Rev. Jerry Falwell's meeting with 200 gays and lesbians at his own church in the fall of 1999 being only the most prominent example. If the right wing decides to cool it on the gay adoption issue, then it may turn out that the American majority that regards homosexual parenting as a "bad thing" could see the same-sex adoption movement as being extreme.

Like gay marriage, same-sex adoption makes the majority of the public nervous. How deep those anxieties go will almost certainly be revealed in the next few years. There is no doubt that the issue of gay adoption is more likely to be decided in favor of the gay community before gay marriages prove acceptable. Gay adoption, for one thing, is less tangled up with religious debates. But the fears of backlash voiced by many gays and some lesbians should not be discounted. The epithet "faggot" is heard too often in school corridors to ignore. "Your father's a faggot" is going to be heard more often, too, as gay adoptions increase. Anyone who thinks that won't mean trouble is being overly optimistic.

Nevertheless, there are more than enough gays and lesbians who want to have a family—or who are mothers and fathers already in spite of their homosexuality—to ensure that the push toward equality with heterosexuals in terms of adoption will go forward. Few gay parents are naïive about the problems they may face going down the line, although they worry about the future more in regard to what their children may face from bigots than they do about themselves.

Gay and lesbian parents are determined to raise their children in the mainstream of American life, and neither doubts expressed within the gay community nor the active opposition of the right wing is going to deter them.

S i x

Gays and Politics

It was not until after Stonewall that anything identifiable as gay politics began to emerge in the United States. Without question, there had always been homosexuals in politics, but their sexual preferences were deeply hidden, to the point that we do not know who most of them were. Many gays assume that James Buchanan, who served as President from 1857 to 1861 and was our only bachelor Chief Executive, was gay. That belief is clearly shared by the hooligans who regularly deface his tomb in Lancaster, Pennsylvania. But there is no evidence to conclusively prove that suspicion, although there were rumors even in his own time.

In more recent times, there were also rumors that Senator Joseph McCarthy, the infamous witch-hunter of the 1950s who claimed that the State Department was infested with communists, was homosexual. We know that his special assistant during this period, Ray Cohn, was gay; his self-hatred was devastatingly depicted in Tony Kushner's Pulitzer Prize–winning play *Angels in America*. J. Edgar Hoover, director of the FBI from 1924 to 1972, was eventually unmasked as a homosexual, but his power and the dossiers he had amassed on public figures protected him from exposure during his long tenure as the nation's chief crime fighter. Other Washington bigwigs were less fortunate. James Forrestal, who had been Secretary of the Navy from 1944 to 1947, and was appointed the first Secretary of Defense by President Truman in 1947, resigned from that position in 1949, supposedly because of illness. But in fact he had been threatened with exposure as a homosexual, and committed suicide shortly thereafter.

A particularly telling example of the difference between the period preceding Stonewall and that following it is provided by Gore Vidal, who ran for Congress in 1960 from the 29th district in upstate New York. In 1948, the twenty-one-year-old Vidal had published his second novel, *The City and the Pillar,* depicting a tragic gay love affair. Vidal's first novel, *Williwaw,* based on his wartime service in the Aleutian Islands, was a success in 1946. But *The City and the Pillar* so outraged the powerful daily book critic of the *New York Times,* Orville Prescott, that he vowed never to review a book by Vidal again. *Time* and *Newsweek* also ignored his next several novels, and Vidal was forced to earn a living writing for television, the movies, and Broadway.

In 1950, Vidal bought a large Greek-revival house, built in 1820 but empty for several years, located on the upper reaches of the Hudson River. It was called Edgewater, and Vidal gradually fixed it up over the next several years. In 1960, the local Democratic Party leaders approached him about running for the district's congressional seat, which had been held throughout most of the century by Republicans. Vidal was handsome, articulate and by then quite famous, particularly for his 1956 Broadway hit, *Visit to a Small Planet*. A new play with presidential politics as its subject, *The Best Man,* had just opened in March of 1960. It didn't hurt that Vidal knew 1960 presidential contender Jack Kennedy and his wife Jackie well. Hugh Auchincloss, Jackie's stepfather, had previously been married to Vidal's mother. It was a sign of a new age that having a shared stepfather was a social plus. But other things had not changed. Vidal ran for Congress from the closet. His scandalous early gay novel was not brought up by his opponent. That kind of smear was hardly necessary. The district was one which, Vidal writes in his memoir *Palimpsest,* "as I tactlessly put it, every four years automatically cast its majority vote for President McKinley." Vidal was a sacrificial lamb, although he did better than any Democrat in decades. But it's especially significant that a man who would later become one of the most outspoken openly gay writers in the country did not even contemplate running as an avowedly gay candidate in 1960.

In fact, it would be fourteen years before an openly gay candidate was elected to even a state legislature. The person to achieve that breakthrough was Elaine Noble, who had worked on Barney Frank's first, successful, campaign for the Massachusetts legislature in 1972. Frank was in the closet, and would not be forced out until the mid-1980s, when he was a U.S. representative. It was Frank's sister, Ann Lewis, the canny political strategist who would ultimately become President Clinton's second term Communications Director, who urged Elaine Noble to run for the Massachusetts legislature from a newly created district surrounding Boston University. Lewis was straight, but she strongly supported gay rights and believed that Noble was exactly the right candidate to break through the barriers to openly gay or lesbian individuals holding public office. Noble was known in the area for her work on down-to-earth issues like housing and health care, and she won handily. But although she was open about her sexual orientation, she did not run as a gay spokesperson or on a specifically gay platform. Even so, simply because she was a lesbian, her election made newspapers across the country.

The election of Elaine Noble had an immediate effect on a closeted gay state senator halfway across the country in Minnesota. Allan Spear had first been elected in 1972. A thirty-seven-year-old assistant professor at the University of Minnesota, Spear, like Noble, had found that it was possible to run successfully on a very liberal platform in a district centered on a large university with a considerable gay population and many students and faculty members eager to push the envelope on social issues. Spear had even endorsed what were then regarded as radical gay activist proposals, including the right of same-sex marriage, which he promised to introduce a bill for if elected. But although some people knew he was gay, and others suspected it, he did not declare his homosexuality either in that election nor during his 1974 re-election campaign. In fact, when a modest bill was introduced in the spring of 1973 that would protect some homosexual rights, it was not Spear but the Roman Catholic majority leader of the Senate, Nicholas Coleman, who took that step. As detailed in *Out for Good,* Coleman had been influenced by the gay brother of a *Minneapolis Star* reporter named Deborah Howell, whom Coleman had fallen in love with after separating from his wife. Spear had not even joined in the debate on the bill, which did not pass, although it did get out of committee to the Senate floor. Spear had continued to feel guilty about his silence, and decided to come out after his 1974 re-election, giving the story to Deborah Howell. It was on the front page of the *Star* the second week of December.

Now Spear was free to put his full weight behind a more extensive gay rights bill that was introduced in the Minnesota legislature in the spring of 1975. The chief behind-the-scenes lobbyist for that bill was gay activist Steve Endean, who had also pressed for the failed legislation in 1973 and succeeded in shepherding a bill protecting the housing and employment rights of homosexuals through the Minneapolis City Council the year before. That bill had not even used the word "homosexual," speaking instead of "affectional or sexual preference." Endean didn't care about language, so long as the legal goal was achieved. He was a master of quiet persuasion, meeting privately with politicians instead of confronting them in public or through the press.

Endean was a classic early example, in fact, of a gay political mainstreamer, working with politicians to achieve set goals, step by modest step. But his goals were not considered sufficiently far-reaching, or his methods aggressive enough, to satisfy more radical gay activists. Although the climate for passage of a gay rights bill at the state level seemed extremely promising, with an influx of younger and more liberal Democratic-Farmer-Labor Party members into the state legislature in the 1974 election, Endean found himself not just trying to corral votes for the new measure, but to control what he referred to as "the crazies" in the gay community. The votes appeared to be there, but once the radicals went to work, they began to evaporate.

The radicals also wanted language that would specifically protect transsexuals and transvestites. They persuaded the Republican minority leader, future governor Arne Carlson, to introduce such language as an amendment, and he spoke movingly about the plight of those who felt trapped in bodies that did not match their self-perception. But even while he was speaking, a group of radical gays in dresses and full make-up were sitting in the public gallery above. That display served only to make wavering legislators nervous, threatening the existing bill.

Out for Good notes that "Steve Endean's careful, conservative, consensus-building plan had turned into a circus," and adds that the experience was one of the "great frustrations of his life." The authors, Dudley Clendinen and Adam Nagourney, clearly sympathize with Endean here. The radicals who insisted upon pressing for a more liberal bill are not denigrated, but Clendinen and Nagourney pointedly declare that the radical "policy of no compromise made sense only if you had the votes. It didn't work if you were trying to *get* the votes."

But from the radical point of view there are two separate problems with this conclusion. First—the general statement that a policy of no compromise doesn't make sense when you're trying to rally enough votes to pass a measure is not always valid in the real world of politics. Certainly, many bills fail at the local, state, and federal level because they try to accomplish too much too soon. Bills in Congress have often been defeated throughout American history because of a refusal to compromise. Sometimes that refusal comes from the liberal end of the spectrum, sometimes from the conservative end. And the same thing occurs right down the line to the city council level in small towns. Yet President Lyndon Johnson, who is still regarded as one of the most powerful Senate Majority Leaders of the century, in either party, once said that the greatest victories were not on bills that passed by sixty votes, but on those that passed by two votes. In such situations, it is often unclear whether the bill will pass or fail until every vote is counted.

In the Minnesota case, the Democratic leader had to call for a vote to defeat the amendment that would have extended protection to transvestites and transsexuals before the more conservative bill could be voted on. Although the amendment was thrown out by considerable margin, it should be remembered that it had been offered not by a radical left-wing legislator, but by the earnest Republican Minority Leader. Moreover, the more conservative bill lost by eighteen votes, 65 to 50, suggesting that it might not have been passed even without the "circus" that supposedly derailed it. Steven Endean may have been too optimistic to start with. And if you are going to lose anyway, why not go for broke?

The second problem from the radical point of view is that incremental progress is simply not good enough. It may be the sensible approach, but it will always mean accepting half a loaf. That will be regarded by most people as better than nothing, but those seeking great changes will not be satisfied. The leader of the contingent of men in drag at the debate, Tom Campbell, had said of the bill that had been voted out of the committee, "It's a problem for a man in a dress." Some will reply to that, "Oh come on!" But this was only six years after Stonewall. And many of those who had resisted arrest with the greatest fury at Stonewall had been men in dresses, drag queens who had had enough from New York City police. The courage of a few men in dresses had been instrumental in starting an entirely new era in gay rights. The gay radicals in Minneapolis were in that sense paying their dues, paying homage to other men in dresses who had battled the police six years before. For some, the reply to Tom Campbell's statement about men in dresses would not be, "Oh come on!" but rather "Right on!"

The split between radical gays who want it all and more politically "sensible" gays who are willing to accept incremental victories, with the hope that in the end, somewhere down the line, they will get it all, has continued to this day. It became strikingly evident in the fight for government funds to deal with the AIDS epidemic in the 1980s, and in the battle over the right of gays to serve in the military in the 1990s. In both small ways and large, it is a split that can crop up at any time, a split that can affect political races at all levels of government. To understand more completely how the political process works—and sometimes fails to work—in respect to the gay rights movement, let's take a look at the career of arguably the most prominent and most effective gay activist working inside the political system, David Mixner.

David Mixner has worked for and helped to elect Democratic politicians from the late mayor of Los Angeles, Tom Bradley, to President Clinton. His efforts as campaign manager, strategist, and fundraiser have given him more behind-the-scenes political clout than any other gay activist in American politics over the last three decades. He was arrested for demonstrating outside the White House during the Reagan Administration in the cause of greater AIDS funding, and again early in the first Clinton Administration while protesting the adoption of the "don't ask, don't tell" policy for gays in the military—although in the latter case, he was invited to a private Oval Office meeting with President Clinton a few months later. To many gays and lesbians he is a hero. Others have their doubts and some actively dislike him. Indeed, his career has highlighted the fault lines in gay political activism. He has been attacked by some militants for not taking a sufficiently hard line even as he has faulted Representative Barney Frank for playing too much of an inside game.

Mixner's 1996 autobiography, *Stranger Among Friends,* tells a story likely to strike chords for any gay man who grew up in a small town in the 1950s and early 1960s. He grew up the son of very conservative parents in rural New Jersey, and felt intense guilt at the realization that he was gay. But he was fortunate to have an older sister with liberal leanings similar to his own. He got an early start in civil rights causes by sending small donations to Martin Luther King Jr., which infuriated his parents, who believed strongly in both charity for poor blacks *and* segregation.

Mixner enrolled at Arizona State University at Tempe—chosen because of his recurring bronchitis—where he organized support for municipal garbage collectors, largely Hispanics, who were trying to unionize. He also had his first gay love affair, with a fellow student who was killed in an automobile accident. Transferring to the University of Maryland, he helped organize student participation in the famous 1967 March on the Pentagon protesting American involvement in Vietnam, and the following winter, became part of the "stay clean for Gene" student army working for Senator Eugene McCarthy prior to the New Hampshire primary. McCarthy's strong showing there influenced President Johnson's decision not to seek a full term, giving the young Mixner a heady taste of the effect of protest politics.

His involvement in the peace movement continued with a major role in organizing the October 15, 1969, Moratorium Day protest against the Vietnam War. By now he was meeting and working with important liberal figures across the country, from the United Automobile Workers leader Walter Reuther to the actress and peace movement stalwart Shirley MacLaine, who would play an important part in his life over the next few years. At a retreat for Moratorium Day workers on Martha's Vineyard in September of 1969, he met a guest of the activist Rick Steans. This new acquaintance "had wiry hair that grew out like an afro," and hailed from Arkansas. His name was Bill Clinton, and the immediate friendship that sprang up between the two young men would, many years later, have major implications for the gay rights movement in America. Even that weekend, Mixner recalls, "As we strolled down the beach arm in arm that day, I experienced for the first time a genuine desire to tell another person about my homosexuality. Clinton's openness about himself and his warm, easy intimacy made me feel safe. But common sense prevailed."

The need for being careful of revealing one's homosexuality in that period was underscored when, while working in the peace movement in Washington, Mixner had an affair with another young man named Frank, who seemed to share all his tastes. Frank turned out to be a "plant" and disappeared just before Mixner was approached by two men with pictures of Frank and himself having sex. They wanted him to become an informant on the workings of the peace movement. Mixner gathered the courage to tell them to do what they wanted with the photos—and for years he expected them to suddenly surface.

Sensing he was under great stress, his colleagues raised the money to send him on his first trip to Europe, where, through Shirley

MacLaine's good offices, he met Vanessa Redgrave in London, and the expatriate "Hollywood Ten" director Jules Dassin and his wife Melina Mercouri in Paris. He was interviewed on the subject of the peace movement by Robert MacNeil, then of the BBC. But most important, he renewed his friendship with Bill Clinton, staying with him at his rundown digs in Oxford, where Clinton was a Rhodes scholar. This was the period when Clinton was struggling over what to do about the draft, and the two friends discussed the war incessantly. A good friendship was greatly deepened.

As should be obvious by now, Mixner has known a great many famous and important people in his life, starting from quite a young age. And that, for some gay activists, is one of the raps against him. To those who are sometimes called "street gays," angry poor young activists whose only recourse is to take to the streets in protest, the David Mixners of this world are inherently suspicious. During the summer of 1999, I talked with a twenty-two-year-old San Francisco activist named Ron who was almost as suspicious of me—"a writer huh?"—as he was of David Mixner, whom he knew all about. "Guys like Mixner can't be trusted," Ron said. "He's got everything, what does he care about the rest of us, really? Oh sure, he's done some good, because he knows how to suck up to the bastards who run everything, but I'm sure he doesn't really tell it like it is. They'd throw him out on his ass if he did."

There is no doubt some truth in this. A great many radical gay activists have been thrown out on their ass over the years exactly because they spoke with extreme bluntness. And that may be of greater service than the radical gays sometimes realize. Their anger and heightened rhetoric in one sense pave the way for someone like Mixner, whose charm, reasonableness, and social graces make politicians and wealthy individuals sympathetic to gay rights say, "Well, at last, someone I can talk with." In all movements for social justice, it may be necessary to have two kinds of people pressing for reform. During the French Revolution, for example, what would Robespierre have been without Danton, and vice versa? In America, during the 1960s, the civil rights movement had need of a Huey Newton to scare people and a

Martin Luther King Jr. to inspire them. It is an old story and it continues to play itself out for the gay rights movement as well.

Certainly David Mixner's smoothness and ability to deal respectfully with political leaders have stood him in very good stead. He moved to California in the early 1970s and set himself up as a political consultant. After serving as campaign manager for Tom Bradley's re-election as mayor of Los Angeles in 1977, Mixner came out to his family and ultimately to political friends across the country, including Bill and Hilary Clinton. Clinton called Mixner after receiving his letter announcing that he was gay and would be working against Proposition 6, the ballot initiative devised by State Senator John V. Briggs to make it illegal for homosexuals to teach in California public schools. "There's nothing ever boring about you, is there?" Clinton said, and went on to say that he and Hillary knew it had taken guts to come out, and that they would always be friends Mixner could count on.

The defeat of the Briggs initiative, modeled after orange juice queen Anita Bryant's successful anti-gay measure in Dade County, Florida, but going even further, initially had 75 percent support in California, and it took a massive effort to turn things around. Harvey Milk ran the campaign against Proposition 6 in northern California and Mixner and his partner Peter Scott, also gay and a sometime lover, headed the southern California effort. It was Mixner and Scott who visited former governor Ronald Reagan in his offices for a meeting set up by a one-time aide to Reagan who was gay, to persuade Reagan to come out against the Briggs initiative. Instead of talking about gay rights, however, Mixner and Scott made the argument that the passage of the initiative would mean that any disgruntled student could create chaos by charging a teacher with being gay or lesbian even if it were untrue. Reagan bought that argument and called for the defeat of the initiative. That was the final stroke needed to rout Briggs.

Some radical gays saw the approach Mixner and Scott took with Reagan as a missed opportunity to make a larger case for gay rights, and there are certainly some who would feel the same way today. Their point of view is not to be dismissed, for as Mixner himself would come to learn in agonizing form fifteen years later, the "inside game" does not always produce good results. If things had gone as they were supposed to, gays and lesbians would have been able to serve openly in the military by the end of 1993. Instead we were saddled with the disastrous "don't ask, don't tell" policy.

Over the years, Mixner had become deeply involved in presidential politics. He had persuaded Gary Hart to appear with the press in tow at a gay fundraiser during Hart's 1984 run for the Democratic nomination—the first time a major presidential candidate had ever openly associated with a gay political group. That did not mean that political skittishness about gays was a thing of the past, of course, even among Democrats. On the East Coast, Steven Endean, now in Washington with the Human Rights Campaign Fund, was able to snare fellow-Minnesotan Walter Mondale, the former vice president and leading contender for the 1984 nomination, to speak at a black-tie fundraiser for the organization at the Waldorf Astoria in New York in 1982. But Mondale managed to avoid saying the words "gay" or "lesbian" and it was only under considerable pressure that he endorsed an end to the ban on gays in the military when he did become the nominee in 1984. Michael Dukakis, Mixner and other gay leaders would discover, was surprisingly nervous about gay issues on the national level despite having courted the gay vote in his campaigns for governor of Massachusetts. For every step forward in terms of gay influence in national politics, there would soon be some backsliding to contend with. And then came Bill Clinton.

Because of his long friendship with Clinton, Mixner inevitably became the chief negotiator for the gay community in dealing with the Clinton campaign. Not that it was a tough job so long as Mixner was able to talk with Bill Clinton directly. As the first baby-boomer to win the nomination of a major party, Clinton had an entirely different attitude towards gay rights than any previous presidential candidate. He was against gay marriages, but otherwise he was willing to support just about every gay rights concern. And his friendship with Mixner was genuine—more genuine, it would later seem, than was the case with a lot of friends Bill picked up in later life. Yet there were still problems. A presidential campaign has layers and layers of advisers. And some of those advisers clearly thought Clinton was getting out ahead of public sentiment on gay issues. There was an awful few days when it looked as though he would not mention gays and lesbians in his acceptance speech at the convention. Mixner and others worked feverishly to get through to Clinton himself that the word gay simply had to be spoken. And in the end it was. Mixner, on the convention floor, finally felt able to let go and celebrate. "We had crossed the finish line," he would write later. "We had won our race."

And Clinton would defeat the sitting president, George Bush, in November. But now came the hard part. Promises, promises—all presidents are faced with a new set of political realities once they are in the Oval Office. Historically, the press would give a new president some breathing room, at least for two or three months. But that didn't happen with Clinton. Things got off to a rocky start with his difficulty in finding the woman Attorney General he promised to appoint, as the spectre of illegal aliens serving as nannies started popping up all over the place. And then came the matter of gays in the military.

Clinton had promised that he would appoint openly gay and lesbian officials throughout his administration, and that part of the bargain was being completely fulfilled, to the great joy of the gay community. But he had also promised to lift the official ban on gays in the military by executive order. He had not wanted to do this right off the bat, but wanted to wait until later in his first year as president. But those in the military hierarchy and in Congress who were dead set against any change in policy started making their feelings known at once. The upcoming battle hit the front page of the *New York Times,* only four days after Clinton had been sworn in. A memo to the President from his Secretary of Defense, former congressman Les Aspin, had been leaked to a *Times* reporter, Eric Schmitt. What Aspin was saying would infuriate gays. He maintained that there was considerable opposition to lifting the ban among the Joint Chiefs of Staff, and warned that if Clinton overturned the ban on gays in the military outright with an executive order, Congress would certainly pass a canceling order. As Commander in Chief, Clinton had a clear right to lift the ban, but having never served in the military himself, he was in a very weak position to engage in an immediate confrontation with the Joint Chiefs.

Over the next several months, the gay community discovered that it had an ever-lengthening list of important adversaries—enemies, many felt—in Washington. There was Defense Secretary Les Aspin, to start with: why had he accepted the job if he was so concerned about implementing a major promise the President had made? There was the chairman of the Joint Chiefs, General Colin Powell, originally appointed by President Bush. As the first African American to become top man in the American military, how could he possibly countenance blatant discrimination against gays and lesbians? Congressional opposition was led by Senator Sam Nunn of Georgia, a man who had come to support civil rights for blacks quite late in the game, and who now seemed to be exhibiting another kind of bigotry.

The liberal press, including the *New York Times* and the *Washington Post,* found themselves in a serious bind. Aspin, Powell, and Nunn were all favorites of theirs, and were regarded as men of great probity and intelligence. All of them, and many others, tried to retain their credentials with the press by saying that gays were undoubtedly fine fellows and lesbians splendid women, and that there was no question homosexuals had served their country with great valor in the armed forces in the past, and that it was clear many must be doing so at the present moment. Senator Nunn went so far as to say that he had had homosexuals on his own staff in the past! Fancy that, said the gay community; why just in the past, did you fire them when you found out they were gay? But the mainstream press wouldn't ask him that question. Editorials in liberal papers suggested that these distinguished gentlemen might be wrong on this issue, but decided as things went from bad to worse to put the most blame on President Clinton. He had been naïve in making such a bold promise in the first place, and now he was being cowardly in not just issuing the executive order and letting the chips fall as they might.

Some sensible citizens, both within and outside the gay community, thought that there was an inherent contradiction here. Was it really cowardly to have second thoughts about a policy if it was in fact naïve in the first place? The mainstream press seemed to be trying to protect its own ass on the same issue by having it both ways. But the great majority of gays were not interested in analyzing the faults of the press, and turned their guns squarely on Clinton himself. Their hero now was seen as having feet of clay. So what if he had already appointed several dozen openly gay or lesbian men and women to positions throughout his administration? The only thing that counted, suddenly, was gays in the military.

There was, of course, very good reason for fury, and for the amnesia about what Clinton had in fact accomplished for gays. Todd, a gay man who was serving in the Army at the time, remembers his feelings vividly. "I was just in a rage. I came from a poor family, and was the last of five kids. My second sister got to college on a scholarship, but she was brilliant, and it was tough sledding for her even so. I wasn't really college material. I did fine in high school, but my real talents were with technical stuff, and the Army seemed the place to get the kind of training I needed, just like recruiters say. I knew I was gay, I'd been having sex with other guys since I was seventeen. But I'm pretty butch, and I thought I could handle the situation. I managed never to get a hard-on in the locker room or the communal showers in high school, I knew how to think about anything but sex in those situations, so I thought I could get away with it just fine."

Todd found that while keeping his sexual impulses under control was not a problem, the behavior of some other soldiers was. "There are a lot of guys in the army, straight and gay, who were grown-ups and minded their own business. But it attracts a fair number of bullies and guys who are still working out adolescent problems. Some of the worst are guys who are always trying to persuade everyone what studs they are. When the argument about gays in the military really got going in 1991, there was a lot of talk about soldiers who were afraid of being groped in the showers by gays. What bullshit. No gay in his right mind is going to do that. And I'll tell you something, the guys who say they are worried about things like that are pretty often turning things upside down. It's not really that they're afraid of being groped—it's that if somebody did grope them they'd get a hard-on. They're really afraid of their own sexual impulses, and they lash out against gays to prove to themselves that they're not 'that way.' There've always been guys like that in the military, and outside it too, but the idea of having gays serving openly scares them shitless, because in that situation they might have to face up with their own sexuality. Any gay guy who's ever served in the military know this, but you can't get the media news to talk about it. I have a friend who gave a reporter the real lowdown on all this, but that part didn't get printed."

Todd says that he has gay friends outside the military who've never forgiven Clinton for compromising on this issue, but claims that gays who are serving in the military at the time were more forgiving. "Clinton got boxed in. If you're in the army you see it happen all the time. He didn't know what he was up against, but boy did he learn fast."

There is no question that Clinton did feel boxed in. He told the gay community that he needed time, after the Aspin memo was leaked, but there was deep unease among gay leaders, including David Mixner. Mixner was among a group of about fifty Hollywood supporters of Clinton who were invited to show up at the Los Angeles airport in late February of 1991 to say hello to the president and rewarded with a tour of Air Force One. Clinton asked Mixner just to give him room to maneuver on the gays in the military issue, but for the first time Mixner wondered about the sincerity of his old friend. As Mixner was leaving Air Force One, a military attache whispered his thanks and asked Mixner to "please keep fighting for us."

Mixner did just that, along with dozens of other gay leaders. Bob Hattoy, the Clinton environmental adviser who had spoken at the Democratic Convention as a gay man with AIDS; Tom Stoddard, the veteran gay rights activist and lawyer who was now the head of the newly-formed Campaign for Military Service; Tim McFeeley, executive director of the Human Rights Campaign Fund; and Tracy Thorne, the decorated fighter pilot who had been discharged because he was gay, were a few of those most likely to be quoted in the press, each of them pressing the case for full openness in the armed services. Because David Mixner had been a friend of the president for a quarter of a century, however, he carried a special burden. If he castigated his old friend publicly, his words would carry special weight, but such a step would almost certainly lose him access to the White House that could prove very valuable on other gay rights issues.

Mixner's decision was in the end made for him by top White House aide Rahm Emanuel. At his first formal press conference, on March 23, Clinton answered a question by saying that he would not rule out the possibility of allowing gays and lesbians to serve openly in the military, but segregating them. This had been how black American soldiers had been dealt with in World War II, and even the suggestion of it caused an uproar. White House spokespeople would not back down on the statement, however, and when Mixner finally talked with Rahm Emanuel, he blew up at Mixner for being so concerned about it. As it happened, Mixner had been asked to appear on ABC's *Nightline* with Ted Koppel that very evening. He went on the air and attacked the very idea of segregating gays in the military, calling it "morally wrong" and "repugnant." He then flew off to Texas to give a speech on the issue, in which he attacked Senator Sam Nunn as the George Wallace of gay rights. This comparison of Nunn with the former Alabama governor who had been an arch foe of desegregation for blacks caused even some gay leaders to blanch, such was Nunn's power. Others thought it was about time someone went after Nunn, who was obviously pulling a lot of strings on the issue.

As he had expected, Mixner's access to the White House was all but completely cut off. He was not even included among a dozen gay leaders invited to the White House to discuss the issue with the president. In that meeting, gay leaders were once again told that, on July 15, as promised, Clinton would indeed sign the executive order ending the ban on gays in the military. That news lent a festive air to the gay and lesbian march on Washington that took place on April 26, 1991. Mixner was even asked to be the keynote speaker at a lunch at the National Press Club for the National Lesbian and Gay Journalists. The scent of victory mixed with the lingering bloom of Washington's famous cherry trees.

And then it all fell apart. In May, it was reported in the *Boston Globe* that Representative Barney Frank was saying he could support what would eventually become the "don't ask, don't tell" compromise that

Senator Nunn had cooked up after his slanted committee hearings in March and April. In his autobiography, Mixner spends two pages discussing Barney Frank, giving him credit for his brilliance and the efforts he had often made on behalf of gay rights issues, both as a public defender of the gay community and a behind-the-scenes operative in Congress. But he also notes that no grassroots gay leader has been spared an angry call from Frank telling them they were asking for too much, too soon. "It seems clear to me that he decided the way to be most effective was being a powerful insider. In many ways, he was right. Having access to the corridors of power can have more of an impact than a thousand marches. In other ways, it has put him at frequent odds with an emerging, anxious homosexual civil rights movement."

This is an extremely significant passage in terms of the gay and lesbian interaction with American politics. I have quoted it to numerous gays and lesbians, and it draws a wide range of reactions. Some say, "I've always thought Barney Frank was really out for himself." Others respond with anger at Mixner: "Where does he get off saying marches don't matter?" The majority of gays and lesbians I talked to, however, basically concluded, "Yes, that's the way it is." Among those not on the front lines there is a strong sense that politics is by its very nature an inside game. Most would also agree that while they particularly like to vote for a qualified gay candidate, straight candidates who are truly strong supporters of gay rights may have more impact in terms of changing the minds of the heterosexual majority. That is not an idea, however, that sits well with a lot of grassroots gay activists. They want gay men and lesbians in office at every level, political gays who are willing to go out on a limb and lose the next election. They want Barney Franks who will sacrifice their political future to gay causes instead of trying to cozy up to the straight establishment. And they think Mixner is too much of an insider himself.

Mixner himself is well aware that "street gays" and some activist leaders don't entirely trust him. That may have something to do with his willingness to get arrested. After the "don't ask, don't tell" compromise was announced by Bill Clinton, despite frantic efforts by gay leaders to head it off, Mixner was one of those to get himself arrested protesting outside the White House, along with such luminaries as Patricia Ireland of the National Organization of Women and the Rev. Mel White of the Universal Fellowship of Metropolitan Community Churches. Mixner subsequently received calls from the White House staffers he had known during the 1992 campaign asking him how he could have made his disenchantment with the president so blatant, and in front of the White House itself! He replied that it was his house, too.

Yet, five months later, Mixner was back in the Oval Office having a one-on-one meeting with Clinton. Pictures were taken of the two of them standing together, smiling. The picture was released to the press. In that meeting, they agreed to disagree, to renew their friendship and work together on the future of gay rights issues, which Clinton reaffirmed his support for. Now, of course, it was time for some in the gay community to say to Mixner, "How could you? How could you even talk to that traitor! And in the White House, too!"

In the years following the "don't ask, don't tell" compromise, President Clinton gradually repaired his relationship with the gay community and its leaders, as well as his friendship with David Mixner. His appointment in 1999 of James Hormel, an openly gay San Francisco philanthropist and meat-packing heir, to serve as ambassador to Luxembourg capped his record as the most pro-gay president in American history. Originally nominated to the post in October of 1997, Hormel's appointment had been fiercely opposed by Republican conservatives and their backers on the religious right, simply because he was gay. Keeping a promise he had made two months earlier to gay leaders, Clinton made a so-called recess appointment on June 4, 1999, while Congress was on vacation. This rarely used executive privilege, an emergency power granted by the Constitution, would allow Hormel to serve as ambassador until the end of the next session of Congress, almost at the end of the Clinton term of office. Hormel thus became the first openly gay envoy in American history, a symbolic victory for gays of considerable import.

That appointment paved the way for Clinton's appearance at a Los Angeles fundraising dinner for the Democratic Congressional Campaign Committee, sponsored by Access Now for Gay and Lesbian Equality and organized by none other than David Mixner. Nearly a thousand people warmly applauded Clinton as he said, "People are still scared of people who aren't like them. And other people are scared of themselves, and they're afraid they won't count unless they've got somebody to look down to, and it must be somebody that is different from you." A week later in New York, Clinton became the first president to speak at a fundraiser for a gay rights organization rather than a political party, appearing at the annual dinner of the Empire State Pride Agenda.

There were still those in the gay community, however, who found themselves unable to forgive the president for making the "don't ask, don't tell" compromise on gays in the military. Instead of protecting gays, it had seemed to make matters worse, as more and men and women were discharged from the armed services as homosexuals—although the Pentagon maintained that as many as a third of those who had identified themselves as homosexual had done so in order to get out of the military early, and insisted, to boot, that some of those who declared themselves gay were in fact heterosexuals manipulating the rules to escape from the service. The entire issue took a new turn in December of 1999, as Private Calvin Glover was convicted by a military court of having beaten a gay soldier, Private First Class Barry Winchell, to death in his bed with a baseball bat—not because Pfc. Winchell had made a pass at Glover, but because he had soundly defeated him in a fist fight brought on by the fact that Glover was continually harassing Winchell about being gay. During the trial, First Lady Hillary Clinton, a candidate for the open Senate seat from New York in 2000, declared that the "don't ask, don't tell" policy was a failure and backed the lifting of the ban on gays in the military entirely. Vice President Gore, running for the Democratic presidential nomination for 2000, had already declared that he would issue an executive order permitting gays to serve openly if elected as president—in line with the fact that, according to David Mixner and others, he had argued against the "don't ask, don't tell" policy in 1991, urging Clinton to fulfill his original promise.

On December 10, 1999, President Clinton himself declared the compromise policy a failure. Some in the gay community began to hope that he would at last issue an executive order permitting gays and lesbians to serve openly before the end of his term. But others were dubious that that would happen, having been burned once, and their doubts were accentuated when the Pentagon announced still another study of the problems the day after Clinton's admission that the compromise policy wasn't working. Studies, as gays have learned over and over again, are the same as delaying tactics. Ironically, on the same day that the new Pentagon study was announced, December 13, 1999, Great Britain declared that it would end its ban on gays in the military in response to a September ruling of the European Court of Human Rights that four gay Britons had been improperly dismissed from the British armed forces because of their sexual orientation. Almost all other European countries have allowed gays in the military for years, beginning with the Netherlands as far back as 1970.

But neither the European model nor the admission that the current policy does not work is likely to persuade most Republican members of Congress to agree that gays and lesbians should be able to serve openly. The Republican Party is far too beholden to the religious right for that; the leading Republican candidate for the party nomination in 2000, Governor George W. Bush of Texas, even refused to meet with the Log Cabin Republicans, the gay political organization that 1996 Republican standard-bearer Bob Dole got in trouble with when his campaign returned a donation from them. (In April 2000, Bush finally met with a group of a dozen hand-picked gays, but the Log Cabin leaders were excluded, and Bush did not change his position on any issue.) If Bush were to be elected president, it is clear nothing would change, and even if Gore became president, Republicans in Congress would obviously attempt to overrule any executive order with a new anti-gay law. Thus it seems virtually certain that this issue, which caused so much unrest in the gay community in the last decade of the twentieth century is likely to remain a thorn in its side well into the first decade of the twenty-first.

Because the issue of gays in the military is necessarily a federal concern, it is a particularly difficult one for gays themselves to influence policy on. While the gay community is very strong in a few big states, its influence is much less apparent in the many smaller ones. Thus, in terms of federal concerns, it is highly dependent on the single person serving as president at any given time, as the events of 1991 proved, and even that may not ultimately be of much help. Presidential politics are very tough and the game is played out in enormously complex ways. The political clout of gays counts for more on the state and local levels, and it is clear that such issues as gay adoption and gay marriage, over which the states have jurisdiction, will be the chief battlegrounds in the first decade of the new century.

But even on the state level, the gay community is finding itself caught up in new internal disagreements that are brought in by its very success. In 1998, there was bitter debate among New York gays about whether to back the re-election of Republican Senator Alfonse D'Amato, who proved himself to be friendly to gays on a number of issues during his three terms in the Senate, or his Democratic challenger Charles Schumer, who had put together a gay–friendly career in the House of Representatives. To have the luxury of making such a choice is a great step forward—yet, the sharpness of the debate in New York did some damage to gay political unity.

The increasing number of openly gay candidates at the local level may also cause future dissension. Following the 1999 elections, the *New York Times* carried a telling article about the election of Daniel Stewart, thirty-seven, as mayor of the upstate town of Plattsburg, New York. Stewart, "a former Air Force Sergeant and tractor trailer driver who now works as a financial clerk at a local car dealership," had become the "first openly gay person to be elected mayor in New York State." A Republican, Stewart defeated a five-term incumbent, after serving on the city council since 1993.

What made the election of particular interest was that the subject of Stewart's homosexuality had not been discussed at all during the election campaign. The incumbent mayor had previously supported such positions as domestic partnership benefits and same-sex marriage, so there was nothing to argue about on those issues, and the campaign turned on such matters as a larger police force and afterschool programs. Even though Plattsburg has only a non-discrimination statute, and no domestic partnership benefit law, the issue was not raised by either candidate. The *Times* quoted the executive director of the Empire State Parade Agenda, a gay lobbying group, as being pleased that sexual orientation had played no part in the race, a view echoed by the Washington-based Gay and Lesbian Victory Fund. The Empire State Group had endorsed Stewart, although it had previously supported the incumbent mayor for his gay-friendly positions. The reason for the switch, however, was not that Stewart was openly gay, but because he was a Republican, and the lobbying group had been trying to find more Republicans to back in order to increase its influence within the state Republican Party.

But although the mainstream lobbying groups the *Times* contacted were happy about the evidence of a "level playing field" for gay candidates that this election seemed to offer, other gays had doubts. I contacted three men who had previously stated that they had no use for candidates who did not actively press for the enactment of issues like domestic partner benefits. The reaction of all three to Stewart was along the lines of, "What good is he if he's not really been pushing our agenda?" One of them pointedly noted that Stewart had told the *Times* that he had been closeted during his eight years in the Air Force. "Okay," he said, "so the guy had to be closeted to stay in the Air Force. I understand that. But he's out now, and if it's more important to him to get elected than to push for things like domestic partner benefits, then he's playing the straight game. He might just as well be right back in the closet. That's progress?"

I suggested that perhaps Stewart would now be in a stronger position to make a push for the enactment of a domestic partnership statute, and that operating behind the scenes did actually work sometimes. "Well, we'll see, won't we," came the reply. "He better damn well do it in his first term. But I don't trust this behind the scenes stuff. I hope you're right, but it wouldn't surprise me to see him move in the other direction in order to get reelected next time, the way Clinton signed that obscene Defense of Marriage Act in '96. I've said it before—I'd rather see a supposedly gay-friendly candidate lose because he stuck to his guns on gay issues. And that goes for an openly gay candidate, too. Keep pressing the issues, win or lose. Having a friend in office instead of an enemy doesn't seem to me to mean a hell of a lot unless they actually do something."

An enemy, of course, can do something that causes actual damage and results in a step backwards. In this particular election in Plattsburg that was not a problem, since the incumbent was also pro-gay. But there are elections where one candidate is truly anti-gay. In that case even most militants say they would vote for even a wishy-washy pro-gay candidate. But still, some believe that more is accomplished by confrontation. Another of the men I spoke with about the Plattsburg election said, "You know, sometimes I wonder if it wouldn't actually do us a lot of good to get a real gay basher like Pat Buchanan in the White House. Then the lines would really be drawn, and we'd find out who's really on our side. It's like racism. There are all these laws to guarantee equality and only a few nut cases are openly racist, but there are millions who still are and are just keeping quiet. We're getting into the same thing with gays. The prejudice has just gone underground, where it's harder to fight."

The notion that having Pat Buchanan in the White House might be a plus in this sense gives the great majority of gays shudders. The spectre of concentration camps for everyone who is HIV-positive is often raised when Buchanan's name is mentioned in the gay community. And to suggest that having such a declared enemy in power may in fact be mere provocation, carrying the role of devil's advocate to an extreme. But the fact that such ideas are put forward by some gays underlines the differences that continue to exist between practical-minded incrementalists and revolutionaries.

When a gay or lesbian stakes out a truly militant position it can sometimes make other guys' hair stand on end. In trying to understand such differences, it is difficult not to think of the career of the great polemicist of the American Revolution, Tom Paine. His famous pamphlet *Common Sense,* calling for American independence from Great

Britain, was enormously influential and certainly helped to create the atmosphere that made the Declaration of Independence possible. But once the Revolutionary War was won, Paine continued to rattle the rafters, to the point that he alienated the founding fathers almost to a man. It took seven years, from 1781 to 1788, to hammer out the United States Constitution, a period during which the new country was governed by a provisional Continental Congress. Virtually every clause was fought over and revised, through a process of debate and compromise that was extremely delicate and required enormous patience. A rock-thrower like Paine was the last person Madison, Hamilton and the rest wanted to deal with. He disapproved of the final result and returned to England, the country of his birth, in 1787, where he published *The Rights of Man,* a ringing defense of the French Revolution. He was promptly accused of treason, fled to France and became a citizen, and was elected to the National Convention in 1792. But he was too much even for the French to handle, and was imprisoned from 1793 to 1794. He returned to the United States in 1802 and died embittered in 1809.

Paine was simply a born revolutionary. Every major social advance in human history has had such figures. Paine is properly remembered as a great man and a true American hero, but he was temperamentally unsuited to dealing with the painful compromise that resulted in eventual stability.

The gay rights movement has had its share of such figures. Larry Kramer is an obvious example. They are important and necessary, but they often end up feeling they've been pushed aside too soon. In the case of winning the war for gay rights, the Tom Paines or Larry Kramers are still needed to push the envelope. But we may have reached a turning point where professional politicians of a more pragmatic kind, from a congressional insider like Barney Frank to a small-town mayor like Daniel Stewart have an equally important part to play. There will be those who regard such individuals as politicians first and gay leaders second, those who equate pragmatism with a lack of courage. And the politicians may view the Larry Kramers with the kind of impatience, even alarm, that Tom Paine engendered in Madison and

Hamilton. "Why can't you show some real guts?" one side asks. "If you don't shut up, you're going to spoil everything!" the other side retorts.

As we begin the new century, there remain many political battles to be fought. Over the next two decades, it seems likely that we will still have need of militant agitators of all kinds. We wouldn't have gotten this far without them, and their voices, even when strident to the point of a scream, can be necessary goads to action. But there is also going to be a need for those who practice conciliation, who know how to consolidate gains already made in a way that ensures those gains will endure. That takes compromise, the willingness to take half a loaf today, and to seek the attainment of further goals slice by slice.

It will not be easy for either side to fully accept the need for the other's input. The consolidators fear backlash. The agitators fear backsliding. Both kinds of fear can be deeply felt, equally genuine, and both have their roots in reality. Pushing too hard too fast can result in lost ground as the resistance of the ignorant and the hate-filled increases. But failure to push ahead with full determination can mean ground never taken, victory lost through overcaution. But it needs to be remembered that one sure way to lose a war is to expend so much energy debating tactics and calling one another names that the reason for fighting in the first place is lost. In politics, nothing gives one side greater pleasure than to watch the other tear itself apart with internal conflicts. The general election is often lost in the primaries because one side has damaged itself so badly in the preliminaries that a final united front is impossible. Those of us in the gay community must recognize that every time we call one another names we give comfort to those who hate, despise, and fear us.

seven

Gays and Religion

In 1977, the Rev. Robert Nugent, a Roman Catholic priest, and Sister Jeanine Grammick, a nun in order of the School Sisters of Notre Dame, founded New Ways Ministry in Mount Ranier, Maryland, in order to reach out to Catholic gays and lesbians. They began conducting workshops, discussion sessions and occasional retreats in an effort present the "compassionate face" of the church to gay and lesbian individuals and also, sometimes, to the Roman Catholic parents of gays and lesbians. Nugent and Grammick were in no way firebrands challenging the dogma of the church, which holds that homosexual acts are "intrinsically disordered." Indeed they were sometimes criticized by gay and lesbian groups for defending the teachings of the church. But although their work had the approval of their immediate superiors, they did not escape the censor of higher church officials.

By 1984, their work was receiving enough attention to alarm James Cardinal Hickey, Archbishop of Washington, within whose diocese they were situated. His criticisms led to their resignations as leaders of the New Ways Ministry, but they continued to hold workshops on homosexuality not only in Maryland, but across the country. That led to what the Vatican would later term "numerous complaints and urgent requests for clarification" from American bishops about the nature of the workshops they were conducting. The two were treading a very fine line. For while the Catholic Church views homosexuality as intrinsically disordered, the catechism also says that homosexuals should be treated with "respect, compassion, and sensitivity." Nugent and Grammick felt that their work was primarily an expression of that kind of compassion, and therefore not at odds with church teachings. But Cardinal Hickey believed, almost from the start, that their efforts were compromised by a "studied ambiguity"—in other words, they were emphasizing the compassion and not saying enough about the fact that the church held the practice of homosexuality to be a sin.

But since the two were not directly contravening the teachings of the church, the Vatican decided to proceed cautiously, and created a commission under Adam Cardinal Maida, Archbishop of Detroit, to determine whether Nugent and Grammick had moved beyond church dogma. (It is not only presidents who create commissions to weigh sticky problems over a considerable period of time; churches do it too.) The commission was formed in 1988. As it pondered the problem and pored over documentation about the workshops and retreats, Nugent and Grammick continued their work. They felt, as did their supporters within the church hierarchy, that the commission would eventually find in their favor, since the Vatican itself had endorsed the concept of "pastoral care" for homosexuals in a 1986 statement. That, surely, was exactly what Nugent and Grammick were involved in.

But in 1994, the two published a book on their ministry, garnering further publicity for their work. The commission met with them after the book's publication, and then sent a completed report to the Vatican. Still no action was taken. The Vatican continued to investigate the issue, largely through correspondence with Nugent and Grammick themselves. This phase continued for three years, from February of 1996 through January of 1999. Six months of silence followed. Then, on July 12, 1999, the Vatican ordered them to end their ministry, on the grounds that they had strayed from the church teachings that held homosexuality to be immoral. They were enjoined permanently from holding any workshops, discussions, or retreats, and indefinitely from holding office within their separate orders. As reported by Gustav Niebuhr in the *New York Times* on July 14, 1999, there was some surprise about the outcome on several fronts. Although Sister Jeannine Grammick declined to comment, the superior at her order, Sister Rosemary Howarth, said, "We are surprised at how severely they came down." The editor of the Jesuit magazine *America,* Rev. Thomas J. Reese, managed to tread his own fine line, saying, "On the positive side, it's clear that the Vatican took a long time before it made its decision. On the negative side, there's very little specificity in the report from the Vatican about what they were doing that was contrary to church teaching." Cardinal Maida, who had headed the original commission, issued a statement hoping that Nugent and Grammick would accept the decision. That hope was echoed by the president of the National Conference of Bishops, but he called attention to the 1986 Vatican statement on the "pastoral care" of homosexuals, and said that such work could and should continue. Here again, there seemed to be a degree of ambiguity. One could minister to gays and lesbians, apparently, but it seemed unclear just how. Auxiliary Bishop of Washington William E. Lori seemed to supply an answer, however, in saying, "Often, errors with regard to faith come from a certain selectivity, and I think this is a classic instance of selecting some of the teaching and distorting the other part." He also reiterated the statements of Cardinal Hickey that "the approach of Sister Jeannine and Father Nugent to the question of immorality of homosexual activity was very ambiguous."

Reading between the lines, it seems clear that what the Vatican wants is for pastoral compassion to be exercised in a context that insists homosexual activity is a sin. Non-religious gays and lesbians have a blunt answer to the idea that both compassion and sinfulness can be emphasized simultaneously: nonsense. But for gays and lesbians with religious faith, the insistence on the part of so many religious denominations that homosexuality is sinful presents a profound problem.

Although the Roman Catholic Church deals with the problem in terms so circumspect that even Catholic clergy can wonder exactly where the balance lies between the offer of compassion and the condemnation of the sin, many Protestant churches are blunter. Thus we get the fundamentalist and evangelical formulation, "Hate the sin but love the sinner." Again, to the non-religious gay or lesbian this can sound like double-talk or outright hypocrisy. But to religious individuals, it is a formulation that must be dealt with. I have talked to dozens of gays and lesbians about this issue, and have found that their approaches to the problem fall into three general categories. Some individuals do not want to even discuss it, and say so flat out. A second group takes what might be called an "ecumenical" stance, suggesting that one can have sincere faith in God without necessarily accepting the dogma of a particular church on all matters. A few people say that they actively challenge the idea that homosexuality is a sin with their own pastors and other members of their congregations.

It is of course impossible to be certain what those who refuse to discuss the issue are thinking, but one comes away with the impression that they try *not* to think about it, using a kind of mental compartmentalization to keep the problem safely locked away. The need to do that would suggest that they find it a troubling issue indeed. Those in the second group have for the most part simply decided to set aside church condemnation of homosexuality as an antiquated idea that has lost its relevance. Ron, a Catholic who grew up in Rhode Island but now lives in Boston, shrugs as he says, "My sister goes to mass every Sunday, and confession once a month, but she ignores the church line on contraception. She and her husband have two kids, and that's all they want. She doesn't even talk about it during confession. Most of her Catholic friends have the same point of view, and I believe the polls show that's a pretty widespread attitude among American Catholics. My sister says the church changes, but slowly, and this just happens to be one of those cases where the laity has gotten ahead of the Vatican. I feel the same way about the condemnation of homosexuality.

Eventually, things will change. I don't worry about it."

Those in the third group are actively pushing for change, whether in the Catholic Church, the Methodist Church, or even in some cases, as Southern Baptists. And those who do push for change are creating a lot of upheaval within their various churches. The Methodist, Presbyterian, and Episcopal denominations have all been in the headlines in recent years because of deep divisions within their churches on issues involving homosexuality, ranging from the investiture of openly gay clergy to marriage ceremonies performed for lesbians and gays. There have been church trials of clergy who were not following church rules, congregations of individual churches have split in half, and in some cases dire warnings of the possibility of general schism have been issued.

The year 1999 proved especially taxing for the United Methodist Church in terms of gay issues. The United Methodist Church is exceeded in size among Protestant denominations in the United States only by the Southern Baptist Convention. It has 8.5 million members, and while widely viewed as a middle-of-the-road denomination, it has always had a powerful conservative wing. Problems about homosexuality surfaced in 1997 when the Rev. Jimmy Creech of Omaha, Nebraska, performed a ceremony of union for two women in his congregation. Creech was tried by a church jury in Nebraska in March of 1998, and narrowly acquitted. His defense was based on the fact that the church rule against homosexual marriages, which had been added in 1996, was placed in the section of the Book of Discipline devoted to social principles, rather than in the section dealing with the structure and specific regulations of the church.

Despite his acquittal, Creech was not re-appointed to his pulpit by his Bishop, and the acquittal was appealed to the Church's high court, known as the Judicial Council. That body concluded in August of 1998 that the rule against conducting union ceremonies for homosexuals was binding. The Rev. Creech vowed to push for the rule to be changed at the church's next General Conference in the year 2000. In the meantime, an old friend from Duke University Divinity School, the Rev. Greg Dell, conducted a service uniting two gay men, one of them a parishioner at his Chicago church. The fact that he did so only a month after the Judicial Council ruling underlined the fact that he was deliberating flouting church rules, and at the end of March 1999, he was convicted by a vote of ten to three by a jury of Methodist clergy. Dell was then suspended, but not defrocked, which was a possible punishment.

The Rev. Don Fado of Sacramento, California, a father of four children and grandfather of nine, was so incensed by the issue that he announced during a sermon that he would like to perform a same-sex ceremony of union, and hoped to draw as many as fifty other ministers to assist. He noted that the couple to be blessed in that ceremony would have to be a special one, because the occasion was bound to draw a great deal of public attention. Two women, Jeanne Barnett, sixty-nine, and Ellie Charlton, sixty-four, who had been together for fifteen years, volunteered a few days later. The women were not only members of the Rev. Fado's church, but also held lay positions within the denomination, serving as a lay leader and a trustee of the California-Nevada Annual Conference, made up of four hundred congregations.

The public ceremony was held on January 1999 in a Sacramento convention center. It was attended by more than a thousand people, and sixty-seven Methodist ministers joined the Rev. Fado in officiating. That placed the church hierarchy in an extremely difficult position. Could they really suspend sixty-eight ministers, as they had suspended the Rev. Dell? On February 11, 2000, the California-Nevada Methodist conference's investigative committee ruled that the complaints were "not proper for trial." The issue is sure to be a divisive one at the 2000 General Conference, the denomination's legislative body that can determine whether the anti-gay language in the Book of Discipline will be left alone, removed, or made stronger.

The depth of the controversy within the Methodist church was further accentuated in June 1999, when a five-thousand-member church in Marietta, Georgia, split over the issue of same-sex marriage ceremonies. But in this case no same-sex marriages had actually been conducted. The split was brought about simply by a vote to allow such ceremonies under certain circumstances on the campus of Atlanta's Emory

University. The ruling was a unanimous one made by the board of trustees of the University. Emory is affiliated with the Methodist Church, and among the trustees voting in favor of allowing same-sex marriages was Bishop Linsey Davis, the head of the North Georgia Methodist Conference, which included the First United Methodist church of Marietta. The pastor of the Marietta church, the Rev. Charles Sineath, himself an Emory alumnus, was incensed by the trustees' ruling, and after some debate, left his church altogether, taking 450 parishioners with him.

There were also political ramifications to the split. One of the parishioners who left with Sineath was Representative Bob Barr, the ultra-conservative Republican representative who led the fight to impeach President Clinton in the House. Speaking for his wife Jeri as well as himself, Mr. Barr told reporters, "We left First United because Charles is our pastor, and we think the very fundamental, Biblical principles he stands for are important." On the other side of the aisle, in more ways than one, Democratic Georgia governor Roy Barnes, remained with the Marietta church. He made no comment at the time about his decision, but an earlier statement made in a speech to the North Georgia United Methodist Conference had made his position quite clear. As reported by the *New York Times,* he said that one of the duties of a Christian was "to be tolerant and forgiving, and unfortunately, many confuse that with weakness."

By the end of 1999, the turmoil within the Methodist church had come full circle, with the Rev. Jimmy Creech once again the center of attention. After being ousted from his pulpit in Nebraska, Creech had spent some time in North Carolina, and there he had married two gay men in April of 1999. Officially under the aegis of the Nebraska Methodist governing body, he was again put on trial. This time he was defrocked by a unanimous vote. He still had the right to appeal to the national body, and made clear that he was not about to back down. "I believe that the law that prohibits pastors from celebrating holy unions with gay and lesbian couples is an unjust and immoral law. Our beloved United Methodist Church has been infected with bigotry. It's bad theology." This was similar to the point the Rev. Don Fado of Sacramento had made the previous October. He had noted then that the Book of Discipline stated that homosexuals were "individuals of sacred worth who need the ministry and guidance of the church." The new rule forbidding pastors to conduct same-sex marriages was, he believed, a contradiction of that statement. The ruling of the church court, he said, "turns around and says you can't give them prayers and blessings."

It is important to understand, however, that the forces for liberalization of the Methodist church, while outspoken, do not necessarily speak for the majority. The *Times* indicated that even many of those who did not leave the Marietta church with the Rev. Sineath were nevertheless in sympathy with him, but felt it was best to remain within the national church in order to combat the idea of same-sex marriage. The divisions have caused some observers, both within the Methodist church and outside it, to wonder if a full schism may not be inevitable, with two smaller national churches emerging from the fray.

Other Protestant denominations have also been roiled by homosexual issues in recent years. The Episcopal Church has long been open to change, and was the first major denomination to approve women as deacons and subsequently as priests. But it, too, has had internal debates about openly homosexual priests and same-sex marriages. In 1996 the retired Episcopal bishop Walter C. Righter was accused of heresy for ordaining an openly gay man named Barry Stopfel as a deacon of St. George's Episcopal Church in upper-middle-class Maplewood, New Jersey. It was only the second heresy trial in the 210-year history of the Episcopal Church. A jury of eight bishops voted to acquit Bishop Righter seven to one, and Barry Stopfel was subsequently ordained a priest. Given the denomination's history of liberalism, it was not a surprising outcome, although at the time it was regarded as a considerable step forward by most religious gays.

The Presbyterian Church has also had problems with the issue of homosexuality. Because of disputes about the ordination of openly gay ministers, which caused a few congregations to split in two, the national church passed an amendment to its constitution in 1997 that required ministers, deacons, and elders "to live in fidelity within the marriage of a man and a woman or in chastity in singleness." This amendment allowed some latitude—an openly gay man could serve the church provided he was chaste. But the new rule was tested in 1999 by an elder of the First Presbyterian Church of Stamford, Connecticut. A graduate of the Princeton Theological Seminary, thirty-eight-year-old Wayne Osborne, was elected to the thirty-member governing board—called a session—of his church for a three-year term. After the end of that term Osborne told his seven-hundred-member congregation that he was involved in a long-term relationship with another church member named Greg Price. Despite this admission, he was then nominated for a second term on the session. Two parishioners protested when his nomination was approved because he had declined to answer a question as to whether his relationship with Price involved sexual activity. He had, however, answered the question, "Are you a self-acknowledged sinner unrepentant of that sin?" by saying that he had not committed any sins that required confession. Because of the challenge by his fellow congregants, however, the matter was referred to five ecclesiastical judges of the Permanent Judiciary Commission of the Presbytery of Southern New England.

On March 6, 1999, the judges approved his eligibility to sit on the session by a vote of four to one. A church deacon, Dan Sassi, explained to the *New York Times* that while the church constitution required the elders to ask about sin, it did not require that "they get a clear answer." He went on to say, "It says that sessions are to respect the right of the individual to decline to answer and not discuss the issue. The other side in this case believes that living with a person is enough proof of sex outside marriage; we say that it is not."

This is a very interesting—and more sophisticated—version of the "don't ask, don't tell" rule that has proved so controversial in regard to service in the U.S. military. Because a full answer is not required even to a direct question, there is considerably more latitude granted. Clearly, however, such latitude is based on a high degree of personal trust. One fellow parishioner, a divorced woman with two children, said the church rule would also apply to her, that it was not a "gay amendment" as such, and that she herself had a great trust in Wayne Osborne to be truthful when he said he had no sin to confess.

Nevertheless, the ruling made in this case does suggest that a person could be truthful if he—or she—did not regard sexual activity outside marriage with a long-term partner to be sinful in the first place. There is some "wriggle room" here.

To the non-religious, the whole concept of theological wriggle room can seem hypocritical. Atheists, too, have their dogma: if you're making choices about what to believe, accepting some things as true and throwing out others, then the whole construct must be false. Yet, for the religious, the questioning of their faith has always been seen as an integral part of the religious experience, from Saint Augustine's "Give me chastity and continence, but not just now," right down to the present day. Augustine's statement tends to particularly annoy many non-religious gays. As Larry, who was raised an Episcopalian and still goes to Christmas services because he likes the music, puts it, "What Augustine really seems to be saying is 'Hey God, let me screw around now and I promise to be good when I get older and I'm not so horny.' Who couldn't get behind that? No wonder death-bed conversions are so popular. It's a bunch of hooey."

Nevertheless, the majority of gays and lesbians I interviewed feel that it is perfectly possible to be both homosexual and religiously devout—even some atheists will grant that much. To those in the gay community for whom religion is a deeply held part of their lives, the debates within their own or other churches can be painful, and can affect them more profoundly than most other issues. Thus they particularly welcome any harbinger of resolution.

One such sign of hope appeared at the end of March, 2000, when the Central Conference of American Rabbis, of Juadism's Reform movement, declared its support for rabbis who wanted to officiate at same-sex ceremonies. Nearly 1.5 million Jews in the United States and Canada are led by the 1,800 rabbis the conference represents, making this the largest group of American clergy ever to vote support for members who conduct gay unions. The individual rabbi was given the right to decide what kind of ritual should be used to bless such a union. The new resolution did not force any rabbi to officiate at gay unions, however; support was also offered to nearly 400 rabbis by a voice vote, there were a number who told reporters afterward that they would not themselves be officiating at same-sex unions, and were grateful for the addition of the language that would support them in that decision. Even those who had reservations about presiding at same-sex unions, however, tended to view the resolution as a "victory for diversity and intellectual tolerance," as Rabbi Clifford E. Librach of Sharon, Massachusetts, told Gustav Neibuhr of the *New York Times.*

Reform rabbis had called for an end to descrimination against homosexual activity between consenting adults as far back as 1977, and voted in 1990 that sexual orientation should not prevent anyone from serving as a rabbi. By the late 1990s, there was even a Gay and Lesbian Rabbinic Network with about fifty members. While the new declaration was entirely in keeping with past progressive steps by the Reform movement, and not really surprising, it was still very encouraging to religious gays and lesbians, whatever their church.

On another and far less likely front, there had been developments the previous year that also heartened many religious gays. On October 23, 1999, the Rev. Jerry Falwell, founder of the Moral Majority and long-outspoken scourge of homosexuality as a sin condemned by the Bible, met his Lynchburg, Virginia, headquarters with two hundred gay Christians. The meeting was arranged in the course of talks that went on for several months with the Rev. Mel White, an openly homosexual minister who heads an ecumenical organization called Soulforce, which promotes religious activity among gays and lesbians. White was once thoroughly closeted, a married man with children. He had so successfully hidden his homosexuality that he was chosen to be the ghostwriter for Falwell's 1973 autobiography, as well as books for Pat Robertson. He had also written speeches for Oliver North. He stunned the religious right when he announced his homosexuality in 1991, and was for many years afterward looked upon by Falwell and the others as an extremely embarrassing "skeleton in the closet"—or, rather, out of it. But despite noisy public debates between the one-time ghostwriter and his former colleagues, Falwell and White continued to talk on the telephone occasionally, and even though such conversations sometimes ended in new acrimony, Falwell never quite slammed the door on White altogether.

Falwell had always maintained that homosexuality was akin to drug addiction or alcoholism, a disease that could be cured. This view had remained in force on the religious right more than a quarter century after the American Psychiatric Association had voted to discard that idea in December of 1973. In 1999, several conservative Republican politicians had started making the disease argument with renewed aggressiveness. Senator Majority Leader Trent Lott added kleptomania to the list of curable diseases homosexuality could be compared to, a suggestion obviously calculated to infuriate gays. A number of political commentators concluded that this new frontal attack on homosexuality was a really a red herring intended to distract conservative Christians from the fact that the Republicans had failed to make any headway in banning abortion. But understanding that a political ploy was behind the new attacks did nothing to assuage the fury within the gay community. And although Senator Lott was widely ridiculed in the press he did not back down an inch. Gays began to wonder how many times the same old dragons had to be slain.

In the midst of this fresh targeting of homosexuals as unrepentant sinners who refused to get help they supposedly needed, Matthew Shepard was murdered in Wyoming. The horrific circumstances of Shepard's death led the press to report other stories about attacks on gays, the incidence of which has historically been underreported. Seizing the initiative, Mel White warned Falwell that the strident anti-homosexuality of the right wing was being seen by some as a sick rationale for violence against gays, and even a goad to such behavior. Unlike Trent Lott, Jerry Falwell has never given the impression of being a stupid man. He listened to his old friend and more recent antagonist, and began to see the need for making some kind of gesture that would stop the talk in the gay community and in the press about the religious right acting as a cheerleader for gay violence.

Falwell and White finally agreed on a format for discussion of the issues involved. White gathered a group of two hundred gay civil rights activists to meet with Falwell and two hundred of his followers in Lynchburg to hash out the differences between them. Both Falwell and White urged demonstrators from their side to stay away. White's pleas to gay activists were heeded. Falwell was less successful in this regard, and several dozen right-wing protestors yelled epithets at the visiting gay rights delegation as they entered the church parking lot. They were led by Rev. Fred Phelps of Topeka, Kansas, who had appeared with some members of his congregation to taunt gays attending Matthew Shepard's funeral.

Nevertheless, the meeting took place in a civil atmosphere once everyone was inside. The gay activists were even more heartened by the sermon Falwell delivered to his church the next day, where they joined more than four thousand worshippers at Falwell's invitation. During his sermon, Falwell reiterated his belief that homosexuality was a sin, but he said, "That has nothing to do with the love factor involved. We are to be lovers of all men and women." The Associated Press quoted the reaction of thirty-six-year-old David Chandler of San Francisco, one of the gay representatives. "His sermon was amazing," Chandler said, "He sent a message to parents to love their children no matter what."

Inevitably, the reaction to the conclave was mixed on all sides. Homophobic agitators like the Rev. Phelps accused Falwell of hypocrisy, and many gays were equally dubious about his motivation. Many gays felt that Falwell was "just covering his ass," in agreeing to tone down his rhetoric, while others took a wait-and-see position. There was general wariness concerning Falwell's sincerity. Editorial comment in the mainstream press was cautious. The *New York Times* saw the meeting as a sign of how far the gay rights movement had progressed, but also suggested that Falwell's "break from bigotry is still incomplete." That, of course, brought letters taking opposite tacks, suggesting on the one hand that Falwell wasn't getting enough credit, and on the other hand that he was receiving too much for basically saying he'd stop advocating lynchings. The middle road often seems to please no one but the Editorialist.

But is there, in fact, a middle road on this subject? If Falwell is still insisting that homosexuals are sinners, many gays will argue that saying it less noisily changes little. "I am a virtuous man, and you're a sinner but I love you even so," is a point of view that has always struck non-religious gays as utter claptrap. Michael, a thirty-two-year-old gay man from a Southern Baptist family who hasn't believed in God since he was eleven, is trenchant on the subject. "My parents believe homosexuality is a sin. That makes me a less good person than they are. I'm double-damned because I won't give up sex or try to become a heterosexual. And they, of course, are doubly good because even though they think I'm a sinner, they still love me because Jesus does. As if they weren't self-righteous enough to start with, they get extra points on the heavenly score board for loving me even though they hate sin. I've told them point-blank that congratulating themselves for loving me despite my supposed sin means they're committing the sin of pride. And that's exactly what's going on with Falwell. This whole business is just another way of patting himself on the back. It reeks of smugness and condescension—both of which have always seemed to me integral to religious beliefs. It makes me sick."

Gays who do believe in God are more willing to give Falwell the benefit of the doubt. Ken, twenty-eight, says, "I not only believe in God, but I also believe he moves in mysterious ways. I think that what has gone on between Mel White and Jerry Falwell over the years, the tug-of-war they've been involved in, is an example of that. Who better to awaken Falwell than the man he trusted to ghost his autobiography? White should be give credit for coming to terms with himself and declaring his homosexuality. And Falwell should be credited for responding to White's efforts to educate him about what it means to be gay. So what if Falwell hasn't come around to understanding the whole story yet? The scales have at least begun to fall from his eyes. I think that's something to celebrate."

But it should be noted that Ken does not share the fundamentalist view that the Bible should be taken literally. It is almost impossible for a gay man to accept the idea that every word in the Bible is God's truth. For gays, the great sticking point in the Bible is the book called Leviticus. The "Leviticus problem" has been dealt with again and again over the years, but it will not go away. Back in the 1970s, both George Weingberg, author of the influential *Society and the Healthy Homosexual*, and C. A. Tripp, author of the best-selling *The Homosexual Matrix*, offered coherent arguments about why the condemnation of homosexuals in Leviticus could and should be discounted. I dealt with the subject in my 1980 book *Straight Women/Gay Men, A Special Relationship.* More recently, Charles Kaiser addressed the controversy in *The Gay Metropolis.* But because when members of the religious right state that the Bible identifies homosexuality as a sin, they really mean that Leviticus does, it seems right to return to the subject once more.

Leviticus is the third of the five Old Testament books of the Pentateuch. They are ascribed by tradition to Moses, but many eminent Biblical scholars and theologians date Leviticus in particular as a much later addition. The book deals with the installation of priests (chapters 8 to 10) and with purity and impurity as they relate to dietary laws (chapters 11 to 16). In terms of this material, Leviticus is described as a "manual instruction for priests," as Oxford's *One Volume Illustrated Encyclopedia* puts it; similar descriptions are found in numerous other reference works.

The injunctions against homosexuality appear in chapters 18 and 20:

> Thou shalt not lie with mankind, as with womankind: it is an abomination. [18: 22 of the King James Version]
>
> If a man lie with mankind, as he lieth with a woman, both of them have committed an abomination: they shall surely be put to death; their blood shall be upon them. [20: 13 of the King James Version]

These are the only specific references to homosexual acts in the Old Testament. The most detailed examination of these two passages was made by John Boswell in his 1980 book *Christianity, Social Tolerance and Homosexuality.* At the time of the book's publication, Boswell, who died in 1994, was the A. Whitney Griswold Professor of History at Yale University. He had spent ten years researching the book, which analyzed records in a dozen languages, and his work was received with great critical acclaim in mainstream press.

Boswell's treatment of the Leviticus question is extremely detailed, turning on both the errors that have crept into translation and the misreading of (or failure to take into account) the historical background.

Suffice it to say that he shows how the word "abomination" distorts and inflates the meaning of the narrower and milder terms (there is more than one) in the original text. He takes note of the fact that even so mild an act as cursing one's parents called for a "death penalty" suggesting a far looser use of the phrase than the idea of actual execution implies. He documents early Christian aversion to the strictures of Leviticus concerning such rules as dietary laws, aversion that has continued down through the ages, meaning that Christian theologians have emphasized the "sin" of homosexuality even as they disregard the dietary laws that were of primary importance to Jews.

Boswell deals in the same way with the New Testament references that in the twentieth century have been "supposed" to use his word, to mean that homosexuals "will be excluded from the kingdom of heaven." These references involve two words in 1 Corinthians 6: 9 and one in Timothy 1: 10, as well as rather vague passages in Romans. Once again, Boswell argues convincingly that these references were not originally intended to cast aspersion on homosexuality as such, but upon sexual looseness in general, including masturbation, and to decry temple prostitutes, both female heterosexuals and male homosexuals, in pagan religions.

While many historians and religious scholars find Boswell's research and arguments to be very solid, fundamentalists and many among the general public cannot be swayed by such "academic" debates. They will continue to believe in what they want to believe—that the Bible says homosexuality is a sin. It is, in fact, easy enough to show that those who claim to believe in the "literal truth" of the Bible often conveniently ignore or downplay Bible passages that could cause them problems. On the level of general behavior, for example, it is always fun to bring up the famous line from the Gospel of Matthew, "It is easier for a camel to pass through the eye of a needle than for a rich man to enter the Kingdom of God." Why then, it can be asked, do so many fundamentalist politicians parade around in eight-hundred-dollar suits? More seriously, it can be noted that fundamentalists have greatly played down the sin of adultery. When Speaker-designate Robert Livingston was exposed as an adulterer in January 1999, most of his congressional colleagues on the religious right were overflowing with sympathy and forgiveness. Why can't they muster a similar attitude toward homosexuals? Because, obviously, they do not want to.

Back in 1981, I appeared on a major morning talkshow in Washington, D. C., for an hour-long discussion of gay men who had previously been married to women and who were often fathers, a subject I had dealt with extensively in *Straight Women/Gay Men*. It was a call-in show, and we heard from a woman who said homosexuals should be stoned to death, "as the Bible says." One of my fellow panelists was a minister, who immediately replied that adulterers should also be stoned to death according to the Bible, and that he doubted that there were enough stones to go around. I added that it was exactly the kind of attitude the woman caller had expressed that drove many gay men to marry despite their sexual orientation, causing potential harm to everyone involved, including any children who might have to deal with their father's eventual coming out.

I have known a number of gay men and lesbians who married because of religious pressures piled on top of social ones, and others whose ability to enjoy sex was severely constricted by their religious guilt. We all have known such people; some readers of this book will have undoubtedly suffered through such conflicts themselves. Indeed, several people I interviewed for this book were obviously troubled by the idea of arguing with "the Bible." Some religious gays and lesbians may feel that it is unseemly to quarrel with the Bible itself, but that should not prevent them from taking issue with those who do not ascribe to all the Bible's teachings themselves but are quick to wield it as weapon against gays. It is not necessary to attack the Bible to confront the hypocrisy of the right wing.

There are also, of course, many gay atheists. Some cultural observers, even within the gay community, think that the percentage of atheists is higher among gays than straights, in part because gays are always being hit over the head with the Bible. Others doubt this, noting that even pollsters will admit that the two subjects they expect most people to lie about are religious faith and masturbation. Atheistic gays and lesbians have solved their problems with religion by rejecting it outright. But that can lead to two problems in terms of the future of gay rights. The first is that even gays who have rejected religion totally cannot really afford to ignore it, since religious tenets lie at the core of our society's prejudice against gays and are central to attempts by the religious right to demonize gays. You cannot ignore artillery aimed in your direction. To some degree, no matter what happens on the legal front concerning gay marriage and adoption, or domestic partnership legislation, there will remain an entrenched bias against homosexuality so long as interpretations of the Bible that emphasize its "sinfulness" are allowed to stand.

The second problem is that the subject of religion so often causes arguments within the gay community itself. In a cover article on hate crimes in the September 26, 1999, issue of *The New York Times Magazine,* Andrew Sullivan noted that in several years of being an openly gay editor and writer, the religious right has never come close to vilifying him as passionately as other homosexuals have. Yet, in the same article he goes after Tony Kushner, author of the Pulitzer Prize–winning play *Angels in America* for an article Kushner wrote for *The Nation* in the aftermath of the murder of Matthew Shepard. In that article Kushner maintained that by their silence about Shepard's murder, and gay bashing in general, "the Pope, his cardinals, and his bishops and priests" were endorsing murder. This is strong stuff, and Sullivan says that it seems to him that Kushner "is expressing hate toward the institution of the Catholic Church, and all those who perpetuate its doctrine." Sullivan is himself a Catholic, while Kushner is Jewish. A reply from Kushner was published two weeks later, in which he said that to point out the failure of religious leaders to respond to a particular issue was not to dismiss the religion in its entirety. Kushner had pointed out in his article—and had been quoted by Sullivan in this regard—that the Pope had declared anti-Semitism a sin. Not to do the same in regard to gay-bashing, in his view, was to "endorse murder."

What do we have here? Is Sullivan objecting to Kushner's view primarily because he himself is Catholic? Do the two men dislike each other personally? Sullivan doesn't actually defend the Pope, he just accuses Kushner of anti-Catholicism. But why doesn't Sullivan say what he thinks the Pope should have done? Is he using Kushner's quote to get across his own discomfort with the Pope's silence on the murder of gays, while avoiding the responsibility of attacking the Pope himself? It is distressing to many gays to see two of the gay community's most eloquent and famous members going after one another in this way. Some gays will side with one man or the other, and argue among themselves, but there are also many who find episodes like this one extremely dispiriting. And there is no question that such incidents do harm to the gay community as a whole. The leaders of the religious right must have been thrilled at this warfare within the gay community.

Ron, the man raised a Baptist who has turned against religion in its entirety, said about this disagreement, "Who cares? Neither of them will come right out and say 'religion itself is evil.' You'll never get anywhere arguing about religion. Just ignore it." This is a common attitude among separatist gays. But there are a large number of gays and lesbians who are devout. They can't "just ignore it." Many such people are trying to educate their own churches on the subject of homosexuality, and insisting that they have as much right to be married within the church or to serve as a priest, rabbi, or minister as heterosexuals do. There is movement towards embracing homosexuals as fully as heterosexuals in many American denominations, as we have seen in this chapter. There is also great resistance, and the debate promises to go on for a long time, possibly for decades. Individual churches are splitting apart on this issue, and there may well be schisms within entire denominations. Changing sacred law is even more difficult than changing secular law.

I grew up toward the end of the period when it was common to say there were two things you did not discuss in public—sex and religion. Sex is now out in the open. Nobody even blinks anymore when the word "penis" is mentioned on television (although the fact that the word can be used on the news may have something to do with declining viewership in parts of the country). But religion remains a problem. Sure it's talked about all the time, but there are a lot of things you aren't supposed to say. Andrew Sullivan obviously thinks that "the Pope endorses murder" is out of line, although the entire point of the article on hate was that nothing can stop it. But for gays and lesbians, sex and religion are intertwined in problematic ways. It is because so many people interpret the Bible as saying homosexuality is a sin that many of our problems exist. A great deal of anti-gay rhetoric is tied directly to religion. It can even seem a kind of Gordian knot—untie it, or sever it, and all else will follow. That means that the interaction between gays and religion is going to be front and center in the coming years.

eight

Violence Against Gays

There were no pictures. But for once the words were enough. They described a slightly built college student, badly beaten, unconscious and tied to a fence on the prairie outside Laramie, Wyoming. The name of the twenty-one-year-old political science major was Matthew Shepard, and the discovery of his brutalized body on October 7, 1998, shocked the nation. Taken to the hospital with severe head wounds, Matthew died five days later. He was openly gay, and the horror of his ordeal put the subject of violence against gays into the headlines and onto the editorial pages of newspapers across the country. *Time* and *Newsweek* carried cover stories. Television broadcast the news of Matthew Shepard's death into a hundred million homes. It was almost impossible not to know what had happened to this very young man who appeared to have been killed just because he was gay.

The nation may have been shocked, but the gay community was not surprised. Violence against gays was too common for that. If you were a gay man who had not met with violence at the hands of gay-hating thugs at some point in your life, you considered yourself lucky. You were bound to have friends who were beaten. It could happen anywhere. It might be a friend who was waylaid on the way home from the one gay bar in a smaller city almost anywhere in the United States. Your friend had been spotted leaving the bar late at night by a couple of drunken toughs. The attack was all too expectable. But another friend would call to say he had been beaten at five-thirty on a summer Friday outside Bloomingdale's in New York City, with lines of people standing in front of the movie theatres across Third Avenue. Often such friends were not in any way obviously gay. You didn't have to be effeminate to be targeted. You could but be dressed like millions of other men, in jeans and a polo shirt. In fact, sometimes you would hear of a man you knew to be straight being attacked. But he was alone, in a place that was associated with gays—a store, a restaurant, a bar, a movie theatre, just walking past but suddenly the victim of other men who hated gays. "Bloomingdale's is full of faggots," they must have said to themselves. "Hey, there goes one now."

If you were attacked, the story was unlikely to get into the newspapers. It was too common, just another item on the police blotter. And you might not have gone to the police in the first place. Depending on where you lived, the police could be almost as hostile as your assailants. You probably wouldn't be beaten by the police unless you were both gay and black, but they could add insult to injury with their sneers. Sure, some cops were fine; there were even cops who were openly gay in the big cities in the 1980s and '90s. But who was sure if you'd get a sympathetic cop or not? And you didn't want the story in the newspapers, anyway, any more than a woman who had been raped did. There was a stigma attached. A newspaper story would just make the whole experience worse in most cases. You might be openly gay, but that didn't mean you announced your orientation to the dry cleaner and the postman. They might assume or even know that you were gay, but things went more easily if they didn't have their noses rubbed in it.

If the news that you'd been beaten did get into the paper, some people would inevitably wonder if you'd asked for it, made a pass at some guy, tried to pick him up to take home for semi-anonymous sex. That question came up in Matthew Shepard's case, of course. It was suggested by friends of the two men who were quickly arrested for the crime, Russel A. Henderson, twenty-two, and Aaron J. McKinney, also twenty-two. But there was a problem with that. They had approached Matthew Shepard in a bar that was known to be frequented by gays, although straights went there too. And witnesses in the bar had told the police that Henderson and McKinney had gone up to Shepard, not the other way around, and that they had then gone outside. If anybody had done any luring, it wasn't Shepard, at least not to start with. Henderson would plead guilty in the spring of 1999 in order to avoid death penalty, but at McKinney's trial in October 1999, his lawyer tried to mount a defense based on the idea that Shepard had made sexual advances that caused McKinney to develop a "five-minute emotional rage" during which he beat Shepard. There were factual problems with this scenario, but they weren't necessary to persuade the judge to throw out such a defense summarily. A sexual advance, he said, was no excuse to murder under any circumstances.

And, in fact, the majority of Americans appeared to see it that way from the start. That surprised many in the gay community, and there was a lot of discussion about why people would feel that way. Was the American public finally beginning to grow up about homosexuality? Were they at least accepting the idea that homosexual desires were not all that different from heterosexual desires, and recognizing that a gay come-on was no more reason for hysteria than a straight come-on? Of course, any sexual approach could be unpleasant to deal with if it was unwanted, and if persistent enough or manipulative enough, could be considered harassment. But there were laws to deal with that problem, and judges were beginning to apply them in same-sex situations as they would in opposite-sex ones. Had the general public gotten the message that there was nothing inherently awful about a gay sexual advance?

That seemed almost too good to be true, from the viewpoint of many gays, and they started looking for other reasons why Matthew

Shepard's case had created surprising sympathy among a broad cross-section of Americans. Part of it obviously had to stem from Matthew Shepard's appearance in photographs. He looked very young, with an open, friendly, boy-next-door expression. Countless Americans must have looked at the picture and seen a grandson, a nephew, a younger brother. The decency and dignity with which his parents, Judy and Dennis Shepard, conducted themselves in the aftermath of their son's murder also had a clear effect. Unlike the parents in several recent murder cases, they did not seek the media's spotlight to rant and rave and promote themselves at every opportunity. Their suffering seemed all the more genuine for not being played out on talk shows. They also made it quietly apparent that they had accepted their son's homosexuality without trauma, and that the fact that Matthew was gay had not altered their love for him. They did not give the impression of loving him in spite of his homosexuality. They just loved him, period.

Those personal factors no doubt helped arouse public sympathy. But there was also a larger symbolic aspect to Matthew's fate. The mental image of him tied to a fence, hanging there for eighteen hours, drenched in blood until he was discovered by a passing bicyclist, could not help but arouse the thought of crucifixion. A beaten young man left to die in the gutter or in a field would have been bad enough. But tied to a fence? There was a degree of cruelty about it that horrified, that made the heart sink and the eyes prickle with what could easily become tears. As in the dragging death of James Byrd Jr. of Jasper, Texas, the previous year, an almost gleeful evil seemed to been at work. King had been black, Matthew gay, but in both cases the men who killed them had obviously been consumed with hate.

There was no hate-crime provision in Wyoming law, but the local authorities made it clear that so far as they were concerned, one was not needed in a case like this. Wyoming has the smallest population of any state in the union, and in popular imagination it retains a cowboy image despite the fact that the state's primary economic product is oil, which was discovered there in the 1860s. But the law enforcement personnel and prosecuting attorneys did not act like cowboys. They seemed to share in the nation's sense of horror, with an added dismay that this brutal crime had occurred in a place they loved. They did not give the slightest hint that Matthew Shepard's sexual orientation excused the crime in any way. At a preliminary hearing, testimony established that Matthew had not made a pass at either Henderson or McKinney, but that even so they kept calling him "queer" and "faggot" as they beat his head with a gun butt. The words of a deputy sherrif spoke volumes about the deep compassion they felt for Matthew. He testified that by the time Matthew's beating was ended, his entire head was covered with blood, except "where he'd been crying and the tears went down his face."

The *New York Times* op-ed columnist Frank Rich quoted those words in a piece titled "The Family Research Charade," subtitled "Gay-baiting post-Matthew." The Family Research Council, which is one of the most virulently homophobic organizations in the United States, is not, as Rich pointed out, "even a quasi-religious organization but a moneyed secular outfit whose leader, Gary Bauer, wants to be president." Rich's article concerned the fact that following Matthew Shepard's murder, "the same groups that worked overtime to stigmatize gay people have mounted a furious propaganda defense to assert that their words and their ads demeaning gay people have nothing to do with anti-gay crimes. Given that these are the same groups that claim the 'pro-gay' rhetoric of Ellen DeGeneres or Joycelyn Elders foments homosexuality, it isn't easy for them to argue now that their words have no consequences. So they instead attack those who call them on their game, hoping that we might be intimidated and shut up."

Did this mean that the gay-bashing forces on the political and religious right were on the run? Not sufficiently, Rich concluded, and went on to wonder what could stop the Family Research Council's crusade against homosexuality if the murder of Matthew Shepard couldn't. But the right wing had always been slow to pick up on signals that its demagoguery has gone too far. Pat Buchanan's "religious war" speech at the 1996 republican convention frightened not only many voters but was subsequently singled out by his own people as a major reason for President Bush's defeat. But that didn't stop Senate Majority Leader Trent Lott from making his infamous speech condemning homosexuality in June of 1998, in the misguided hope that such an attack would get religious conservatives to the polls in that fall's congressional elections. Historically, the party of the sitting president loses seats in a mid-term election, but instead the Democrats picked up some house seats and held their own in the Senate in November. That election came, of course, a month after Matthew Shepard's murder. Were the voters telling the Republican right to shut up about issues like homosexuality? There is no way of knowing the answer to that, but there were numerous commentators who thought it was part of the larger picture, and even some moderate Republican officeholders, like Senator Arlen Specter of Pennsylvania, suggested that the "culture war" approach was not helping Republicans.

Throughout 1999, many individual gays and lesbians began to think that perhaps the murder of Matthew Shepard had begun to change things. "It's not something I can prove," said Marsha, a lesbian on the staff of a Democratic state senator in Maryland. "But this is a curious state, one that leans Democratic but has a strong conservative element and a lot of very religious people. I get the feeling that people are sick of the culture wars. They don't want to hear people spewing hate. There's an old lady in my neighborhood whom I only knew slightly, and I'd never had a conversation with her about my sex life, that's for sure. But after Matthew Shepard was killed she stopped me on the street and told me how terrible it was. She's a Southern Baptist, and I thought, hey, this means something. It's subtle, but I think it's there."

If Marsha is right, that subtle change can only have been given a further small push forward by the words Mathew Shepard's father spoke on November 4, 1999, at the sentencing hearings for his son's killer, Aaron J. McKinney. Referring at one point to his son as "my hero," Dennis Shepard said, "Matt has become a symbol, some say a martyr, putting a boy-next-door face on hate crimes. That's fine with me. Matt would be thrilled if his death helped others. . . . Matt's beating, hospitalization, and funeral focused worldwide attention on hate. Good is coming out of evil. People have said 'enough is enough. . . .' Mr. McKinney, you've made the world realize that a person's lifestyle is not a reason for discrimination, intolerance, persecution, and violence.

The is not the 1920s, '30s or '40s of Nazi Germany. My son died because of your ignorance and intolerance. I can't bring him back. But I can do my best to see this never, ever happens to another person or another family again. As I mentioned earlier, my son has become a symbol, a symbol against hate and people like you, a symbol for encouraging respect for individuality, for appreciating someone who is different, for tolerance. I miss my son, but I am proud to say that he is my son. . . .

"I would like nothing better than to see you die, Mr. Mckinney. However, this is the time to begin the healing process, to show mercy to someone who refused to show any mercy, to use this as a first step in my own closure about losing Matt. . . . You robbed me of something very precious and I will never forgive you for that. Mr. McKinney, I give you life in memory of one who no longer lives. May you have a long life and may you thank Matthew for every day of it."

After his conviction for second degree murder on November 3, 1999, Aaron McKinney was eligible for death by lethal injection, and the agreement arrived at overnight by which he would serve two consecutive life sentences and give up the right to appeal in return came as surprise. As Dennis Shepard made clear, he and his wife had consented to the agreement. This was obviously difficult for them to do, but it was an act of mercy that carried it's own symbolic value in the battle against hate crimes. A spokesperson for the Human Rights Campaign, the largest gay rights group in America, David M. Smith, reacted favorably to the sentencing agreement, saying, "Gay and lesbian Americans can now have renewed faith in our justice system. We can only hope a strong message was sent, that in America hate crimes will not be tolerated and that there are severe consequences for violent, hateful actions."

Gays in general were receptive to the sentencing agreement, particular since their greatest fear about the trial had been put to rest at the start by Judge Barton Voight. The "gay panic" defense that the court-appointed defense attorneys had tried to introduce was a worst-case scenario so far as most gays were concerned. If the defendant in this highly publicized case had been able to argue that his claimed sexual abuse as a child had triggered his attack on Matthew Shepard, because Matthew had supposedly come on to him, it would have served as a rationale for other such attacks. There had been other cases in which the defense had argued that the attacker so feared his own homosexual tendencies that he lost control when advances were made by another man. Such a defense suggests that fear and prejudice give the attacker a right to commit violence. In trials involving racial hatred, that kind of defense is not allowed. To allow it in a trial involving hatred for gays is to stigmatize the victim. The fact that Judge Voight disallowed such a defense, in spite of the fact that Wyoming has no hate-crime law, was extremely reassuring to the gay community, and set a strong precedent for future cases in other states that have not passed hate-crime legislation. Thus, right at the start of the trial an important victory for gay rights had been achieved, and the magnanimous sentencing agreement took place in a context that had already established the heinous nature of violence against gays.

Both symbolically and legally, therefore, the Shepard case created a new atmosphere in the country. Within the gay community there is both sadness and residual anger that it took the horrific beating death of Matthew Shepard to achieve such progress. And the question remains as to how much of a deterrent to violence against gays the life imprisonment of Henerson and McKinney will prove to be. Attention spans are short in our society, and hatred abounds. The fact that the anti-gay hatemongers led by Rev. Fred Phelps of Kansas City showed up to shout epithets at Matthew Shepard's funeral suggests the depth of the hatred that exists. Such demonstrators did not show up at the trial, however. That may not mean that anti-gay forces are truly cowed, but it does suggest that they have recognized that public sympathy is not with them, for now. Whether the Shepard case will make it more difficult for people like the Rev. Phelps to attract followers is yet to be determined.

Some in the gay community are optimistic, believing that a corner was finally turned with the Shepard case. Malcolm, a thirty-five-year-old architect from Chicago, puts it this way: "I was beaten in 1996 by three guys who came charging out of nowhere while I was walking with a friend. He happens to be straight, but it was late at night and we were laughing. What were laughing about is interesting. We're both Chicago Bulls fans, and we were talking about the buttons at the Democratic convention that substituted Dennis Rodman's name for Hillary Clinton's middle name—Rodman instead of Rodham. So we were talking about basketball and politics, not some drag queen's get-up or the size of somebody's basket. I might have been talking about those subjects with someone else; I love drag-queens and it just kills me that loose pants have been in vogue so long. But no, it was basketball. If the guys who attacked us had been listening they might not have assumed we were gay, everybody knows that gays don't like sports, right? But it was dark and we were two good-looking guys laughing. Pow! We were both in good shape, and the thugs got out of there pretty fast. We just had a few bruises. But that attack kept me nervous for some time, and it really bothered my straight friend. He couldn't believe it was happening. When Matthew Shepard's verdict came in, he called me up and said, 'Hey, want to go for a late night stroll?' And I feel the same way, a little safer. Maybe I am making too much of it, but it seems to me there's a change in the air. Sure the haters are still out there, I guess they always will be. But I think that on the whole we're getting there."

Other gays are extremely skeptical. "I think violence against gays will get worse," says Aaron, a twenty-nine-year-old graphic designer. "Incidents have gone up in a lot of places since Shepard was killed, not down. The general public may be more aware of the problem, even a little more sympathetic, but it wasn't the general public you had to be afraid of in the first place. The haters aren't going to stop hating and I think they're going to act out their hate even more as gays become more accepted in general. If you go by the theory that haters are really afraid of something in themselves—and I do—then they're going to become even more fearful as homosexuality is more accepted. That just shoves them in the corner, and people who are cornered are dangerous. It's not a rational thing, and the life sentences for Shepard's killers won't make them think twice. Capital punishment doesn't keep people from killing, that's a law-and-order myth, so why should life sentences do the trick? Of course the judge was right to throw out the gay panic defense, it shouldn't be allowed, but that doesn't mean it isn't real. It's no excuse, but it's there. And it isn't rational. So I think that we'll see a lot more anti-gay violence in the next twenty years. It may be a last gasp kind of a thing—you can hope for that—but in the short term I think we're going to have a lot of trouble."

There is plenty of evidence to support Aaron's pessimism, and his reasons for it. In Fort Collins, Colorado, where Matthew Shepard was taken to the Poudre Valley Hospital after he was found tied to the fence outside Laramie, Wyoming, the two gay organizations, the Lambda Community Center and the Rainbow Chorus, received e-mail messages the day after Matthew's death. The messages were identical, and concluded with the statement, "I hope it happens more." And police departments across the country, from New York to Houston, reported increases in incidents of violence against gays during the first half of 1999. There have been suggestions that such increases are due to the fact that more gays are actually reporting such physical attacks, but that is entirely hypothetical. What's more, there are many places where gays would hesitate to report such an incident. In September of 1999, for example, the Associated Press reported, the sheriff of Lee County, Florida, posted a letter on his official government web site to "denounce abortion and attack homosexuals, feminists, atheists, and the American Civil Liberties Union." He labeled these as the "diabolical forces of moral corruption." That's more of an incitement to anti-gay violence than an invitation to report such incidents. And while this kind of open antagonism may be rare, gays across the country say that they would be reluctant to report an attack to the police. Many gay men say that if they could get up and walk away after a beating, they never would report it, especially if they live in a small town or secondary city. "Are you kidding?" many men said to me.

Even among young people in this country, much remains unchanged. A report by James Brooke in the *New York Times* at the time of Matthew Shepard's murder detailed numerous studies showing the extent of anti-gay harassment and outright violence in schools and colleges. A 1997 study of four thousand high school students in Massachusetts revealed that 22 percent of the gay respondents had stayed home from school in the previous month because they were afraid of being attacked. Thirty-one percent had actually been hurt or threatened with injury at school in the course of the previous year. Some heterosexual students had stated that they had stayed home or been injured or threatened at school, but the number of homosexual students who had had such problems was five times as high.

More disturbing still were the results of a study carried out by a forensic psychologist named Karen Franklin, a researcher at the University of Washington. She conducted a study in 1988 of five hundred community college students in the San Francisco area. Thirty-two percent of the male respondents said they had verbally threatened homosexuals. And 18 percent stated that they had "physically threatened or assaulted" homosexuals. The willingness to admit such behavior is in itself alarming, suggesting that these young men felt little guilt about having aggressive feelings towards gays. It could be assumed that the numbers were even higher, but some did not want to admit what they had done. Of course it is also possible that some who admitted such behavior were boasting, inflating their egos by admitting to "macho" acts they did not actually commit, but such a conclusion would in itself suggest that being anti-gay was a perfectly acceptable, even admired, stance among their peers. It is noteworthy, of course, that these results were obtained in San Francisco, a city in which gays are a powerful political and cultural presence. That fact tends to support the commonly expressed idea that greater acceptance of gays and lesbians by the general public makes some individuals feel more threatened than ever, and increases their anti-gay behavior.

It's also important to remember that it is not just gay men who are subject to threats and actual assault. Lesbians are at risk too, and more so in recent years. Historically, as has often been noted, lesbianism has aroused less fear and animosity among the general public than male homosexuality. Two women could walk along the street holding hands without attracting the kind of suspicious animosity that two men doing the same thing inevitably attracted. (At least in America; in Italy, heterosexual men think nothing of strolling arm in arm.) It is significant that E. M. Forster completed his autobiographical gay novel *Maurice* in

1914, but did not allow it to be published until after his death—it appeared in 1971—while Radclyffe Hall's *The Well of Loneliness,* with its lesbian narrator, Stephen Gordon, became an international best seller when it was published in 1928. At the same time that the public was accepting the lesbianism of Gertrude Stein and her lover Alice B. Toklas in the 1930s, Cole Porter and Noel Coward were at some pains to disguise their homosexuality. This does not necessarily mean that lesbians had an "easier time of it" than gay men in the first half of the century, but by and large lesbianism did not upset the public to the degree that male homosexuality did. When I was growing up in Andover, Massachusetts in the 1940s and '50s, there was a wealthy local woman, a famous gardener, who always wore velvet pants tucked into calf-high boots, and a velvet beret. It was explained to me when I was about seven that "Bessie likes to think of herself as man." But she was accepted everywhere, and there was very little sniggering, even among children, perhaps because she had an innate dignity that was impregnable.

But with the simultaneous rise of feminism and gay rights in the 1960s and '70s, lesbians became a favorite target of right-wing politicians. Partially this was an obvious attempt to "smear" the women's rights movement in general. That was an especially successful ploy in the Deep South, where raising suspicions about sexual "deviancy" was a time-honored technique. When John F. Kennedy's future best man, Representative George A. Smathers of Florida, ran against the liberal Claude Pepper (later the great champion of the elderly in Congress) for Senator in 1950, he told his redneck audiences in the Florida panhandle, "My opponent is a practicing homosapiens and his sister is a thespian." Pepper's sister was indeed an actress and Pepper a member of the human race, but these unfamiliar words had their desired effect with the hicks, and Smathers won handily. But in recent years, right-wing demagoguery against gays and lesbians has clearly fueled vicious attacks against lesbians as well as gay men. As recently as 1998, Regan Wolf was brutally whipped, knocked unconscious, and tied spread-eagled to her porch twice in seven months near Lancaster, South Carolina. During the first attack, a message was also spray-painted on her front steps: "Jesus weren't born for you, faggot."

A prominent South Carolina minister, the Rev. Stan Y. Craig of Greenvile, has called homosexuality a "stench in the nostrils of God." In a front page article in the *New York Times* in July 1998, reporter Kevin Sack detailed the fierce resistance to the gay rights movement in South Carolina. He noted that there was widespread agreement not only among gay rights leaders but also social scientists and government officials that "a distinct confluence of factors has contributed to the rawness of gay rights conflicts here: the pervasiveness of fundamentalist Christianity, which interprets scriptural warnings against homosexuality as God-given truth; the ties between religious conservatives and the state's surging Republican party; the increasing activism of the state's gay community; the South's history of institutionalized bigotry, and the state's resistance to cultural change, racial and otherwise."

Special note should be taken of the phrase "the South's history of institutionalized bigotry" in the above paragraph. Many blacks object to comparisons between the movement for black civil rights and the movement for gay civil rights. In part, this is because black civil rights are seen in the context of slavery, and it is felt that gays have not suffered discrimination of equal historical dimensions. This is in some ways a legitimate distinction, but it can be tinged with the same kind of attempt to claim exclusive martyrdom that causes some Jews to play down the killing of gays in Nazi concentration camps. And at times, there is clear homophobia at work in the black community. It has never been forgotten by gay rights activists of the 1970s that Black Panther leader Eldridge Cleaver often spoke of "faggots" as a threat to America, and that some black radicals still take a similar line. In a state like South Carolina, moreover, there is no question that there is a connection between the open racism of the past and the gay bashing of the present. In the *Times* article, Harriet D. Hancock, co-chairwoman of the South Carolina chapter of Parents, Families, and Friends of Lesbians and Gays, a woman with three children including a gay son, put it bluntly: "There may be discrimination against gays and lesbians everywhere, but here the gay-baiting is so open. It used to be race-baiting. Now it's gay baiting."

But while the gay-baiting forces in South Carolina are sufficiently virulent to attract notice from the national press, it is clear that they do not reflect a consensus on the subject. Numerous Republican politicians, including former governor David Beasley and U.S. Representative Bob Inglis, have made clear their opposition to gay rights. Yet in the 1998 elections, Senator Ernest F. Hollings, who had sponsored a bill in the U.S. Senate in 1983 to protect homosexuals from employment discrimination, was narrowly re-elected despite the issue made of that vote by his opponent, Representative Inglis. Thus it is incorrect to suggest that the state as a whole is homophobic. It is, however, a current hotbed of anti-gay bigotry, and the viciousness of the rhetoric is reflected in the brutal beatings of Regan Wolf.

In looking to the future of gay rights, it is sometimes difficult to decide which is more of a problem, the open gay-baiting at the highest political levels that takes place in a state like South Carolina, or the almost casual homophobia that infects American society nearly everywhere. In terms of casual homophobia, an interesting study was made in Des Moines, Iowa, by a group called Concerned Students in 1997. They conducted ten "homophobia recording days" at five high schools. Recording comments made in both hallways and classrooms, the group established that the average high school student was likely to hear about twenty-five remarks every day that were clearly anti-gay. While Iowa is situated in the "American Heartland" usually associated with a degree of social conservatism, it is also a state with exceptionally high educational standards, first in the nation in terms of the number of high school graduates who go to college. It has some of the most conservative and some of the most liberal constituents in the country, and its voting pattern resembles those of the country as a whole. That make its presidential caucuses, which have traditionally begun the primary season, more germane than some might think. At the same time, however, its reputation for educational excellence, and the broad range of political opinion to be found within its borders, make it all the more disheartening that casual homophobia should be so prevalent.

These facts underline the question of where and how we can best combat homophobia in the years ahead. In some ways, the kind of overt bigotry now so much in evidence in South Carolina is easier to fight. Its very virulence attracts the attention of the national media, and thus can be directly challenged. Elsewhere in the South, the homophobic statements of its Mississippi Senator and Republican Majority Leader, Trent Lott, were countered by newspaper editorials across the country, and his views were discussed on many television programs. In such cases as well, one derisive comment from Jay Leno, David Letterman, or Conan O'Brien can serve to put someone like Trent Lott in his place more effectively than a dozen high-sounding editorials. In such situations, gays can sometimes be almost grateful for the existence of highly placed bigots. On the other hand, the casual remarks made in the corridors of high schools in Des Moines—and high schools everywhere, for that matter—may represent a deeper and more intractable problem.

There is always a question as to the relationship between casual bigotry and actual violence committed against a minority group. Despite all the laws against overt racism, for example, there is no question that America remains deeply infected with racial distrust and disdain. The civic house has been spruced up and given a fresh coat of paint, but there are still insidious termites within its walls, and they can surface at any time. Yet outright violence against blacks has waned. When it does occur, as in the dragging death of James Byrd Jr., the broad public seems genuinely sickened by it. The murder of Matthew Shepard appears to have had a similar effect on the public, to a degree not previously evident in cases of violence against gays. That revulsion carried over to the murder of Pfc. Barry Winchell in July of 1999. The military trial of his killer, Pvt. Calvin Glover, in December of 1999 attracted major media attention. In part this was because of larger concerns about the role of gays in the military, but again, great emphasis was placed on Winchell's human worth. The statement by Pvt. Glover, following his conviction, that Winchell was a better man than he, had considerable impact. Even if it was made as part of a plea for forgiveness, it was another step toward the recognition that a gay man can indeed be a superior human being, more worthy than many straight men.

We may be entering a stage in the education of the heterosexual majority that will bring about a decrease in the violence against gays and some lesbians that went unheeded for so long. That in itself would be a major step forward in the long struggle for the full recognition of the human worth of homosexual men and women. But we will still need to worry about the termites below the surface. Eradicating them will be a task requiring our steadfast efforts well into the twenty-first century.

nine

An End to Homophobia?

One spring day in 1961, I was having lunch with a group of friends in the large paneled dining room of Lowell House at Harvard College when a provocative question was asked. One of our group said, out of the blue, that he had a game for us to play. "If you were going to have sex with a man, which person at this table would you have it with?" He suggested that we go around the table, one by one, and answer the question. Someone insisted that he should start, and he did, naming me, which was of course flattering. And then we all answered the question in turn. Nobody seemed nervous about it, there was no giggling at the answers, and three others out of eight picked me also. I found it an enjoyable experience.

I wasn't out, exactly, although my three roommates, all of whom were present, knew I was in love with a beautiful student a year younger who wouldn't "do it," even though most people thought he was also in love with me. But no one else at the table was out in any way. Three of them were certainly straight, and I gather they're all grandfathers by now. Another, whom we all suspected was probably gay, remains closeted to this day, so far as anyone knows. One subsequently went through a gay period but has been married for years, while one of my roommates (whom I had chosen in the lunch-table game) got married, had two kids, got divorced and finally came out. The young man who asked the question was John Berendt, author of the phenomenally successful best-seller, *Midnight in the Garden of Good and Evil.* I haven't seen John in thirty-five years, although I kept up with his career in publishing, and was delighted with the success of *Midnight,* a book I enjoyed enormously.

I bring up that long-ago lunchtime game at Lowell House not merely to boast about my youthful attractiveness. (A friend who's twenty years younger than I am recently looked at some old pictures of me and said, "You were quite something back then. . . ." Un-huh.) Memories of that lunch came flooding back in the spring of 1999 because of an article that appeared in *Harvard Magazine*, the college alumni publication. The article by Andrew Tobias, titled "Gay Like Me," brought an avalanche of mail to the magazine, much of it supportive, but some of it angry and vituperative. What stunned me was that some of the strongest anti-gay statements came not from men who had graduated from Harvard in the 1930s, '40s and '50s, but from men who had graduated after the group gathered in Lowell House in 1961. Some old-timers were shocked, some not, but the fear and bigotry that showed up in letters from men younger than I was quite astonishing. There were, of course, many anti-gay bigots at Harvard in my time, and I'm sure there are still quite a few, but I was surprised that men who had graduated in the 1960s and 1970s were still displaying their bigotry so openly at this late date. If products of a famously "liberal" college can celebrate their hatred of gays with such unabashed fervor, the extent of the problem we still face in seeking full acceptance from the straight majority becomes clearer and more daunting.

There was one negative letter about Tobias's article that was no surprise at all. It came from the poisonous pen of Charles W. Socarides, M.D., who received a Harvard degree in 1945. Socarides signed his letter, "President, The National Association for Research and Therapy of Homosexuality." A psychiatrist, Socarides has been claiming to "cure" homosexuality in some patients for decades, and has recently been taken up by those on the religious right who maintain that we gays and lesbians could all "straighten out" if we'd just submit to behavior-altering shock treatment. He was one of the most vociferous opponents of the 1973 vote by the American Psychiatric Association to remove homosexuality from its list of mental disorders, one of the most important gay rights victories ever attained. Socarides's claims of curing homosexuality have been thoroughly debunked and, irony of ironies, his son Richard not only came out as a homosexual but also served as a liaison to the gay community for President Clinton. Not even that could shut dad up, however. The fact that twenty-seven years after the APA changed its classification of homosexuality, Socarides is still insisting we're just mentally ill, and still has too many followers, is another indication of a continuing problem.

The unpleasant truth is that although the gay rights movement has had some remarkable successes, considering where matters stood in 1969, before Stonewall, the day has still not arrived when we can even debate whether the glass is half full or half empty. Polls show that only a third of the public even accepts that homosexuality as a state of being that people are born into, rather than a choice of "lifestyle" or wayward course that young people can be seduced into embracing. In 1993, a six-page report in *Science* by the geneticist Dean Hammer and his associates made headlines around the world suggesting that a "gay gene" had been found. But that was usual press sensationalism. As Hammer explained in his 1994 book, *The Science of Desire,* a genetic marker connected to male homosexuality had been found, but a great deal more work needed to be done—and he took great pains to note that not everyone with this genetic marker would turn out to be gay, and that some without it might be so. The great majority of gays and lesbians are entirely certain—"know" is not too strong a word—that we were born gay. But the scientific proof of that personal certainty may lie years in the future. What's more, the media quickly turned to the question of whether it would be eventually be possible to alter the supposed gay gene in the unborn, or at least have the choice of aborting a fetus that carried the gene. There was even a Broadway play on the subject, *The Twilight of the Golds* by Jonathan Tolins. In other words, the discovery of a genetic marker for homosexuality metamorphosed into a debate about the morality of eliminating the existence of future homosexuals. This was not an encouraging development, to say the least.

Or was it? A Broadway play about the ethics of how homosexuality should be dealt with? This was certainly very new territory, and while the play itself was not a success, it had enough merit to be filmed as a cable TV movie starring such well-known actors as Faye Dunaway, Jennifer Beals, Jack Klugman, Rosie O'Donnell, and Brendan Fraser. Fraser, a rising star who has proved himself remarkably unafraid of gay themes, played the openy gay brother of Jennifer Beals, who was pregnant with the potentially gay child. What's more, the story was essentially an old-fashioned comedy-drama about a squabbling family who happened to be dealing with a futuristic concern. The gay brother was given the most telling speeches, in defense of homosexuality. Thus the fact that such a play could even find backers for a Broadway production, amidst the mega-musicals and revivals that dominate its stages, is an indication of serious changes in public attitudes toward homosexuality in general.

Thirty years after Stonewall, we find ourselves in a transition period in terms of the way gay subjects are presented to the public and within "gay culture" itself. To those of us who came of age in the 1940s, '50s, and early '60s, the differences can seem staggering. For younger gays it may be difficult to grasp how much it meant to discover the existence of a novel like Gore Vidal's *The City and the Pillar,* which despite its tragic ending at least confirmed that there were other young men who were attracted to their own sex. I remember the excitement with which I read daring new novels like James Baldwin's *Giovanni's Room* (1956) and *Another Country* (1962), or Christopher Isherwood's *A Single Man* (1964), in which he finally shed the role of sexless narrator he had first adopted in his Berlin stories of 1939. His original "Herr Isherwood" would finally become openly gay in the movie version of *Carabet* (1972), embodied by the always luscious Michael York, who had already assayed the bisexual central character in 1970's *Something For Everyone,* a movie that retains a good deal of its amoral piquancy even today. There was a thrill that accompanied these encounters with open representation of Oscar Wilde's "love that dare not speak its name," that has vanished in a time of Internet porn.

In the 1950s, gay men read *The Diary of a Flea,* that "dirty book" from the eighteenth century, and the novels of Henry Miller. They were about heterosexual exploits, but they described erect dicks and copious ejaculations in detail. They were more explicit than John Rechy would be in his 1963 novel *City of the Night*. In the early 1960s, living in Europe, I bought an elegant green paperback issued by Olympia Press. Everyone was talking about the scene in William Burroughs's *Naked Lunch* where two male trapeze artists sucked each other off as they whirled through the air. What a coup it was when I was asked by the managing editor of the *Transatlantic Review,* Heathcote Williams—very cute and thoroughly straight—to cook lunch for Burroughs at the review offices. Burroughs was dressed like a banker and as a dignified as one, which was quite disappointing, although he did give me his sincere compliments for my *Sole Veronique*. Heathcote, who was about to be famous for his book on the speakers in Hyde Park, took me several times to dingy private clubs in London that were open during the afternoon when the pubs were closed. He would point out some gentleman in tweeds and whisper that he was Lord so-and-so. "He's gay too," Heathcote would say, smiling at me. Those words were always nice to hear, back in those days, when you kept counting gays like sheep. Let's see, how many do I know now?

But I wasn't really surprised anymore. There seemed to be gay men in Europe wherever you looked. I could walk hand in hand in Rome with my lover, since straight men did it too. On Ibiza, the island in the Balearics where I'd spent nine months, there were as many gays as straights among the foreign colony of three thousand. The Left Bank in Paris was teeming with American and English gays, and American blacks were also there because no one gave them a hard time. In London, there were two very important men in their fields who would take me and my lover out to lunch at the kind of restaurant where they were bound to run into someone they knew. And it wasn't that they were openly gay—it would be several years before the Wolfenden Act, which decriminalized gay sex, would be passed. They just didn't worry about appearances. One of them was married with two children, and invited me and my lover for a weekend with his family in the country, where we were put in a double bed.

America was another story. When I returned from four years in Europe at the end of 1965, I could almost smell the fear in New York. On the Continent you could purchase European porn magazines with little difficulty. In New York, you felt somewhat furtive when buying even the physique magazines featuring the jock-strap clad Jim Stryker at the Mom and Pop newsstand at the corner of 83rd and Columbus. A wealthy collector actually whispered, in his own apartment, as he showed me his rarest prize, a remarkable photograph of Roddy McDowall performing auto-fellatio. It would be years before I learned that Roddy was more than willing to demonstrate this neat trick on top of the piano at Hollywood parties, charming the ladies and astounding the men.

In the years just prior to Stonewall, gays had their bars and there was plenty of activity at the baths, but these were, in a way, secret places that existed in another dimension. There were certain restaurants gays frequented, and others you went to with straights or a not-too-butch lesbian friend in tow. I remember being invited to dinner at the splendid East 30s duplex of an extremely handsome young editor for whom I had done a book-doctoring job. He first introduced me to his sexy roommate, also in publishing, and then made a considerable production of showing me a large bedroom with a king-sized bed where one of them supposedly slept, and a virtual closet with a single bed occupied by the other, I was told. We spent the entire evening trading gay clues look back and forth but getting nowhere close to the truth, and it took a second dinner before the admission was made that we were all cocksuckers.

Then came Stonewall, and things began to change. The radical gays and early leaders of the political movement led the way, but while some of us who were not organizationally minded also became increasingly open, millions of other gays were cautious for a long time. I was doing a lot of ghostwriting in the early 1970s, and I was at some pains to make my sexual orientation known as soon as possible to the people I was working with. I was sick of playing games with people who might be nervous—I'd basically been out for years, but had sometimes been reticent in employment situations. No longer. Paul was even blunter in dealing with fellow cast members when he started rehearsals for a new show. Because he is very straight in his appearance and behavior—he wouldn't have been starring as Papa Charlie in *Shenandoah* otherwise—even gays in the cast sometimes assumed he was heterosexual. To ward off crushes by the ladies in the cast, and make things clear before I showed up on a visit to share his bed, he would announce, very casually, and with a disarming smile, "Hi, I'm Paul. That's right, I 'm a cocksucker." We have straight women friends from Paul's years in the theatre who are still grateful to him for that—they'd fallen for too many guys who turned out to be gay after getting involved with them.

But even in the 1970s, the majority of gays and lesbians were still in the closet, or out only under the right circumstances. AIDS brought a great many more gay men out—although people like Paul Popham were still managing to infuriate Larry Kramer at the height of the crisis by worrying about being "known." And as more gays came out, the heterosexual majority began to realize that there are an awful lot of queers wandering around. Like Europeans, they began to get used to the idea that same-sex love, or just plain same-sex lust, was too common to get all that upset about. But that's not quite right, is it? What was happening was that some segments of the straight majority were getting used to the idea. Some always had been—in show business, or in the university world—to a degree at least. But now there were doctors and lawyers and corporate executives who were almost ready to say, "Gay, so what?" It depended to some extent on where you lived. The South was a major problem, except in big cities, or university towns, or the odd home to general eccentricity like Savannah. Parts of the Midwest and the Mountain states were problems, and like much of the Bible Belt, they still can be. And in too many of those places, those who fear homosexuals, who find the idea of male/male or female/female sex not only immoral but physically repugnant, are politically and socially powerful. The haters are not going to give up easily.

But the anti-gay factions, the ones who want to fight us tooth and nail, have a serious problem to face as we enter a new century. The problem is not just the courts that have started handing down decisions that favor gays on issues like gay adoptions or gay marriage. There have been too few such decisions yet for anti-gay forces to get panicky about. They've even managed to counter decisions in favor of gay marriages in Hawaii and Alaska. Nor is the problem the fact that city councils and state legislatures are increasingly passing laws to protect gays and lesbians from discrimination. The large majority of small cities and towns, the places where the most fervent gay haters live, have no such laws. Less than a third of the state legislatures have passed such laws so far. Politicians can be threatened or bought off with considerable ease even now. Yes, there is turmoil in a number of religious denominations as ministers decide to marry same-sex couples. But they are few in number, even if the press is starting to give them a lot of attention. They're just wayward mavericks, aren't they? Containable, despite the fuss that creates? So the gay hater hopes.

But, oh, the press, moan the gay haters. The media. Television. Movies. Why are newspapers and magazines and television paying so much attention to gay issues? Well, sensationalism sells, of course. But why doesn't the media emphasize the gay aspect of a serial killer like John Wayne Gacy out in California a few years back? They treated him just like that guy Bundy who killed all those women. Well, can't control the news. Can you? Not when you've got a president who makes it okay to say "penis" on the air. "Damn that Clinton anyway," the gay haters say. "First he appoints all those fags and dykes to federal office and then he makes it necessary to broadcast the word 'penis' in your living room. . . ."

And you've got women kissing women in prime time. That dreadful Ellen DeGeneres, and of course Roseanne had to get into the act. You can see men kissing on cable channels! And, dear God the movies! That nice Greg Kinnear playing a fag, a saintly fag, in *As Good as it*

Gets. And he's straight, you could tell he's straight, he didn't even swish. Then they have to give an Academy Award nomination to Sir Ian McKellen, who's come right out and said he's queer, for that movie about the fag director. William Hurt? Oh, we forgot about him, he actually won for playing a fag in *Kiss of the Spider Woman*. And that was years ago, what 1985? Well at least he swished.

▼ ▼ ▼

There is a reason why conservative politicians want to take us back to the 1950s, the golden age of conformity, that sweet time when almost everybody was in the closet. The gay haters are fighting a losing battle when it comes to the media. Gays are everywhere, all of a sudden, and a great many of them are sympathetic. In the Julia Roberts hit of 1997, *My Best Friend's Wedding,* even straights tended to find her gay confidante played by openly gay Rupert Everett more sympathetic that the object of her affections, Dermot Mulroney. That kind of character in that kind of romantic comedy does more to undermine fear of homosexuals than any number of eloquent speeches by gay leaders, or dozens of books by academics that are read only by gays and intellectual straights who support gay rights. A brilliant treatise like John Boswell's *Same-Sex Unions (In Premodern Europe)*, which provides convincing evidence that the Roman Catholic and Eastern Orthodox churches once sanctioned such unions, has no effect on right-wing gay haters—it is too easily dismissed as the work of what George Wallace liked to call "pointy-headed intellectuals." But popular culture does penetrate the consciousness of the "average American," sometimes directly, sometimes subliminally.

There are many gays with a different point of view, who have difficulty seeing how important popular culture is to future progress. There is a tendency for some gays to focus on a particular tree to the degree that they lose any real sense of the forest. For example, there were gays who did not like William Hurt's Oscar-winning performance in *Kiss of the Spider Woman* because they thought he was too "swishy," and thus continuing a long tradition of stereotyping gays as effeminate. It didn't matter that the effeminacy of the character was essential to the point. Others were angry that a great role was played by a heterosexual—despite the fact that there were no major openly gay stars around to play it. Now we have Rupert Everett, who might indeed be good in the role. But there were gays who were annoyed that Everett played his part in *My Best Friend's Wedding* so straight, thus failing to live up to the challenge of charming the straight audience with a more flamboyantly gay approach. This kind of second guessing is very much with us in reactions to the television series *Will and Grace*. Some gays love it and see it as a great step forward (at least for television). Others loathe it, seeing one male lead as too straight, or the other as too swishy by far, a debate that can become quickly tiresome. The fact is that straights as well as gays are watching it in sufficient numbers that it got a second season. And to watch it is to become used to "being around" openly gay people. It is an old truism of network scheduling to ask whether the home-viewing audience will want to ask the characters in a new series into their home. Well the two gay men on this show have been asked. Dottie, a social worker who counsels teenagers, including a number of gay and lesbian kids, says, "Hey, listen up! That show offers not one but two gay role models of different kinds. It's not Chekhov, it's just a sitcom, for God's sake. At least they're here. And that helps my kids. It really does."

Part of the problem is that gays and lesbians have far more mixed feelings about gay role models than many in the gay community like to admit. If you start asking probing questions on this subject, the answers quickly start canceling one another out. What everyone really seems to want is a role model that's close to a clone of their own selves. They're often not looking for a role model as much as they are for validation of what they already are, and that covers a lot of territory. More butch radical gay men, more drag queens, more butch lesbians, more sweet sensitive lesbians, more handsome corporate gays who could pass for straight, more loving lesbian moms. Sometimes you can get a truly confounding answer like, "I'd like to see a lesbian who's like Mary Tyler

Moore," or "I'd like to see a sexy, masculine guy like Brad Pitt." It can make me want to say, "Check the Internet. Brad Pitt's on there in the nude someplace." And he is—a friend sent me a copy.

The point here is that whether or not we in the gay community find our perfect gay or lesbian image in television or in the movies, gay and lesbian characters are close to becoming a staple. So what if a lot of them are people you or I wouldn't want to have over for dinner, let alone go to bed with. A vast straight audience is now seeing gays and lesbians all the time. They're getting used to them. Eventually, if we're lucky, the novelty will wear off and they'll start seeing them as people instead of gay and lesbian people. Just people. Beautiful people sometimes, and homely other times. Nice people sometimes, and nasty people sometimes. Just like the heterosexuals on television and in the movies.

For many gays and lesbians, the ultimate objective is to be seen as just people, good, bad, and indifferent people, no better or worse than the general run of human beings, and not all that different, either. Gay mainstreamers clearly want that to happen. But gay separatists do not have the same goal. They want the same legal rights as the heterosexual majority, but they want to be accepted for their differences, not in spite of them, and they certainly don't want to be considered just like everyone else. For the gay separatist, "gay pride" means pride in being different, sometimes with the spoken or unspoken implication of being better.

It is time to finally bring up a phrase that causes no end of debate, and on occasion no little acrimony: "gay sensibility." When I was a sophomore at Harvard I came out to a friend from Radcliffe, Joyce Smith, who is now known to a wide readership as the mystery novelist Joyce Christmas. Joyce is straight, but she has had many gay friends; for years she was an AIDS volunteer, not just helping to raise money but visiting numerous dying men in the hospital, often men she'd never met, but whom I have no doubt quickly came to regard her as a friend. She is that kind of person. I told her I was gay as we were sitting on the far bank of the Charles River, looking back across at the Harvard Houses. It was a lovely spring day. I told her that the only thing that worried me much about being gay was that it might limit me as a writer—a stupid worry for someone who admired Andre Gide as much as I did, but we're all young once. Joyce shook her head. She told me she had suspected I might be gay because I seemed to understand women too well for a straight man, especially one so young, and said that she thought that being gay would be a plus because I saw things that other people did not.

That, in its most romantic sense, is what is meant by many people when they use the term "gay sensibility." But for a lot of gays, that's not what it means at all. It can mean any of several other things that sometimes overlap, but can also be quite discrete from one another. It can mean having sex as often as possible with as many partners as possible in a celebration of erotic freedom. It can mean being a Judy Garland fan. It can mean making witty, contemptuous remarks about the pathetic treadmill on which "breeders" spend their lives. It can mean having more exquisite taste than any heterosexual, male or female, ever dreamed of—and, if you're lucky, making the straight world pay through the nose for your clothes or designs. It can mean being a drag queen, inhabiting your own special Oz. And there is no way to shoehorn all these meanings into a single way of living in the world, or coming up with a coherent list of political objectives to satisfy this diversity of self-definitions. Try as you may, you won't be able to blend all these clashing colors into any kind of perfect rainbow in the sky.

So instead, we get fights in the paintshop. Depending on what is going on at the moment, the fights can range from the plain silly to matters of life and death. I'll leave the silly examples to the reader's imagination—nobody will have problems coming up with a few favorite cat fights, although one reader may be on one side and another in opposition. (In other words, I sometimes know when to keep my mouth shut.) But the bitter debates that went on as the AIDS crisis escalated certainly qualify in the life-and-death category.

At the moment, as we move into a new century, the most heated debates concern gay marriage and gay adoption, and the general movement of many gays toward further integration with mainstream American life. Various points of view on these issues have been presented throughout the book. But there are other aspects of the divisions between mainstreamers and separatists that should be touched on. The split in the gay community, particularly between gay men of different views, are apparent in male porn movies, for example. In the 1970s and 1980s, there were many more porn films featuring clean-cut, often beautiful men like Kip Noll than there were gritty leather-oriented movies starring the likes of Al Parker. (Straight readers will have to take my word for it—both men were legends of gay porn.) The pretty young men, sometimes quite effeminate, who ruled the roost in that period, were often referred to derisively as "twinkies" by those who preferred their men butcher and their sex raunchier. But in the last several years there has been a reversal. Raunch and leather are in and "twinkies" are definitely out. I've known a few straight women who were quite enthralled with some of the earlier movies, even finding a few beautiful. They do not like the raunchier ones that predominate now—they're too brutal, too animalistic.

Bart is a producer of porn movies. He went to an Ivy League college, and is straight. He started out with straight porn, but has found gay porn to be more lucrative. "You don't have to pay a male star as much as a female star," he notes, "with a couple of exceptions who aren't worth the money in my opinion." Bart thinks the shift to grittier male porn has come about because the market is now being driven by gays who want nothing to do with the mainstream. "There are gay men who see themselves as being 'above porn' now. They are busy proving themselves to be good, solid citizens. And the gays who really like porn want to be raunchy so they can draw a clearer line between themselves, the real gays, as they see it, and the mainstream gays."

This may be too simplistic. I know a lot of mainstreamers who like leather porn, too. But some of them do seem to regard such films as a sort of secret vice—just like many consumers of heterosexual porn, they seem to take a certain naughty pleasure in thinking, "If only the neighbors knew what was going on behind my white picket fence." It does seem significant that the rise in leather porn has coincided with the increase of slick "general interest" gay magazines in which nobody's genitals are shown, the ads are from the same companies you'd see in *Gourmet* (though sometimes with a gay slant), and movie stars grace the covers. But even within the pages of these quite sedate publications you can see the tensions within the gay community.

Out, for example, which is very slick indeed, does run a column by writer Dan Savage that manages to stir up the magazine's readership to a stinging buzz. Savage is a gay father who's had the temerity to wax poetic about his son's penis and his boyfriend's ass. The letters fly, accusing him of giving gays a bad name just when decorum is needed to cement the gains that have been made in recent years. A gay father writing about his son's penis? "My God," the letters say, "what's that going to do to the fight for gay adoption when the right wing gets ahold of it?" Most of the letters about Savage's column take him to task for courting a backlash, but there's always someone to defend him, saying, "We're different, the straights are going to have to live with it."

Both the letter writers who attack Dan Savage and the ones who defend him have valid concerns—if you step back and consider their points calmly. Many third-way gays understand that there is a good reason for mainstreamers whose chief concern is gay adoption or gay marriage to worry about backlash. Support for these issues among the general public is thin enough as it is, and it's more subject to erosion than expansion. The two-thirds vote against gay marriage on the ballot initiatives in Hawaii and Alaska make the situation abundantly clear. Support for gay adoption is somewhat stronger, but by no means solid. And backlash could come with the swiftness of a lightening bolt. One major news story about an adopted child being sexually abused by a gay parent could do enormous damage—it wouldn't matter that heterosexual genetic parents sexually abuse their children at alarming rates. There is plenty of reason to worry about backlash.

But third-way gays and lesbians can also sympathize with the gay separatists who say, "We're different from straights. We really do live in the world in another way. Stop with all this picket fence stuff, it's a snare and a delusion." Gay pride, the cry that we have a right to be treated with respect even though we're different, got us going on the path toward liberation. There is an emotional logic to the sense that we haven't yet attained enough respect for our differences to start selling out to mainstream middle-class values.

Can gays and lesbians have it both ways? Can we as a larger community work to persuade the general public that all of us deserve respect and legal protection, those who want to marry a same-sex partner and have children and those who want nothing of the kind? It ought to be possible. After all, the heterosexual world is increasingly divided along similar lines. The number of single households rises with every census. Marriage has lost a lot of its traditional appeal even for straights, and multiple marriages are widely accepted as a new norm. There is no longer a monolithic way of living in the straight world. Surely gays and lesbians have the right to a similar latitude.

But curiously, within the gay community, divergent ways of seeing the world and of living in it give rise to great anger. It is strange that human beings who are so different from the majority in terms of their sexual orientation can get so upset that people like themselves in sexual terms want to live out their lives in different ways. We demand respect for being different, but too often are intolerant of difference within our own community. If we truly expect to achieve legal and social parity with the straight world, we are going to have to begin to respect one another more, as gays and lesbians who don't live the same way as other gays and lesbians.

Historically, gay radicals and gay negotiators have both been necessary to the progress we have made in the last three decades. Sometimes the moderate gays who have a knack for talking to politicians in secluded offices have been the heroes and heroines of the gay rights movement, the ones who have gotten legislation passed and open homosexuals appointed to public office. When they have dropped the ball, because of complacency or overcaution or simple fatigue, the radicals have taken to the streets and gotten things moving again. We have needed one another in the past, and it seems certain that we will again in the new century we have entered. We have a long road still to travel, but it seems important to recognize that it is a relay race as much as a marathon. From time to time, we are going to have to pass the baton back and forth.

There are many, especially among third-way gays, who are by their very nature less vocal, who think that many of the violent arguments that erupt within the gay community are largely a sign of continued insecurity. There is plenty of reason to be insecure. I remember back to that lunch in Lowell House in 1961, when a group of young men, some straight and some gay, were willing to pick a putative sexual partner from those at the table, and I celebrate that moment as an astonishing step toward a new kind of life. At the time, I could hardly believe it was happening. But then, nearly forty years later, I read the words of hate about gays that appeared in the *Harvard Magazine,* and I thought, "How little has changed for some people." I had come such a long way, so many gays and lesbians I knew had come so far—grown and prospered and come to terms with themselves and the world. But here were these hateful letters from people who had never grown up.

There are too many hateful letters being exchanged within the gay community itself, as well. How can we hate people who are so like us, fundamentally, when we are asking the great American public to accept us despite—or even for—our differences?

Maybe the main thing we have to do in the twenty-first century is to grow up ourselves.

Bibliography

Baird, Robert M., and Stuart E. Rosenbaum, eds. *Same-Sex Marriage.* Amherst, New York: Prometheus Books, 1997.

Baker, Ronald. *Private Acts, Social Consequences: Aids and the Politics of Public Health.* New York: Free Press, 1989.

Bawer, Bruce. *A Place at the Table.* New York: Poseiden, 1994.

Bawer, Bruce, ed. *Beyond Queer.* New York: Free Press, 1996.

Bell, Arthur. *Dancing the Gay Lib Blues: A Year in the Homosexual Liberation Movement.* New York: Simon & Schuster, 1971.

Boswell, John. *Christianity, Social Tolerance, and Homosexuality.* Chicago: The University of Chicago Press, 1981.

———. *Same-Sex Unions in Premodern Europe.* New York: Vintage Books, 1995.

Browning, Frank. *The Culture of Desire: Paradox and Perversity in Gay Lives Today.* New York: Crown, 1993.

Burroughs, William. *The Naked Lunch.* Paris: Olympia Press, 1959.

Callen, Michael. *Surviving AIDS.* New York: Harper Perrenial, 1990.

Clendinen, Dudley, and Adam Nagourney. *Out for Good.* New York: Simon & Schuster, 1999.

Cory, Donald Webster. *The Homosexual in America*. New York: Greenberg, 1951.

Dew, Robb Forman. *The Family Heart*. Reading, Massachusetts: Addison Wesley, 1994.

Duberman, Martin. *Stonewall*. New York: Dutton, 1994.

Eherenstein, David. *Open Secret*. New York: William Morrow, 1998.

Gunderson, Steve, and Rob Morris, with Bruce Bawer. *House and Home*. New York: Simon & Schuster, 1999.

Hammer, Dean, and Peter Copeland. *The Science of Desire*. New York: Simon & Schuster, 1994.

Harris, Daniel. *The Rise and Fall of Gay Culture*. New York: Hyperion, 1997.

Hay, Harry, ed. Will Roscoe. *Radical Gay*. Boston: Beacon Press, 1996.

Isherwood, Christopher. *A Single Man*. New York: Simon & Schuster, 1964.

Jay, Karla, and Allen Young. *Lavender Culture*. New York: New York University Press, 1994.

Johnson, Fenton. *Geography of the Heart*. New York: Scribner, 1996.

Kaiser, Charles. *The Gay Metropolis*. New York: Houghton Mifflin, 1997.

Klaich, Dolores. *Woman Plus Woman*. New York: Simon & Schuster, 1974.

Kopay, David, and Perry Deane Young. *The David Kopay Story*. New York: Bantam, 1977.

Kramer, Larry. *Faggots*. New York: Random House, 1978.

———. *The Normal Heart*. New York: New American Library, 1986.

Loughery, John. *The Other Side Of Silence*. New York: Henry Holt, 1998.

Lowenthal, Michael, ed. *Gay Men at the Millenium*. New York: Tarcher/Putnam, 1997.

Malone, John. *Straight Women/Gay Men: A Special Relationship.* New York: Dial Press, 1980.

Marcus, Eric. *Making History: The Struggle for Gay and Lesbian Equal Rights 1945-1990*. New York: HarperCollins, 1992.

Marotta, Toby. *The Politics of Homosexuality.* Boston: Houghton Mifflin, 1980.

Mixner, David. *Stranger Among Friends.* New York: Bantam, 1996.

Monette, Paul. *Becoming a Man*. New York: Harper Collins, 1992.

———. *Borrowed Time: An AIDS Memoir.* New York: Harcourt Brace Javanovitch, 1988.

Nava, Michael, and Robert Dabidoff. *Created Equal: Why Gay Rights Matter to America*. New York: St. Martin's Press, 1994.

Rechy, John. *City of Night*. New York: Grove Press, 1964.

Shilts, Randy. *And the Band Played On*. New York: Penguin, 1988.

———. The Mayor of Castro Street: *The Life and Times of Harvey Milk.* New York: St. Martin's Press, 1982.

Signorile, Michelangelo. *Queer in America: Sex, Media and the Closets of Power.* New York: Random House, 1993.

Simpson, Ruth. *From the Closets to the Courts.* New York: Viking, 1976.

Sullivan, Andrew. *Virtually Normal*. New York: Knopf, 1995.

Teal, Donn. *The Gay Militants.* New York: St. Martin's Press, 1994.

Tripp, C.A. *The Homosexual Matrix*. New York: New American Library, 1976.

Verghese, Abraham. *My Own Country: A Doctor's Story of a Town and a People in the Age of AIDS.* New York: Simon & Schuster, 1994.

Vidal, Gore. *The City and the Pillar.* New York: Dutton, 1948.

———. *Palimpsest.* New York: Penguin, 1996.

Weinberg, George. *Society and the Healthy Homosexual.* New York: Anchor Books, 1973.

White, Edmund. *States of Desire.* New York: Bantam, 1981.

Woods, Gregory. *A History of Gay Literature.* New Haven: Yale University Press, 1998.

Made in the USA
Coppell, TX
24 January 2022